PRIESTESS PATH

PRIESTESS PATH

13 POWERFUL LESSONS TO BUILD YOUR INNER STRENGTH

STACEY DEMARCO

ROCKPOOL

I wish to dedicate this to all the priestesses in my life past and present.

A Rockpool book
PO Box 252
Summer Hill
NSW 2130
Australia

rockpoolpublishing.com
Follow us! **f** 🅾 rockpoolpublishing
Tag your images with #rockpoolpublishing

ISBN: 9781925946161

Published in 2023 by Rockpool Publishing
Copyright text © Stacey Demarco 2023
Copyright design © Rockpool Publishing 2023

Edited by Brooke Halliwell
Design by Sara Lindberg, Rockpool Publishing
Author photo by Stu Nairne

A catalogue record for this
book is available from the
National Library of Australia

Printed and bound in China
10 9 8 7 6 5 4 3 2 1

I had been training for this night.

I stood barefoot under the big moon, looking up, feeling moonstruck right down into my bones. I knew that humans had done this same thing for millennia after millennia. I felt deeply that we humans had done this since we were able to stand up on our hind legs. I stood in the footprints of women before me. I was humbled.

Rationally, I recalled that archaeologists and sociologists don't know how long we have been experiencing state changes through engagement with the lunar and earth energies, but it's an ancient thing. This feeling is old. Really old.

I had bathed in salt and herbs and dressed in new clothes. A fire had been lit. Resins burned. Songs sung.

The priestess who I had worked with for the last two years washed my hands with water and then poured a little oil on my palms.

She said the words.

I answered in a tongue not my own but one I had learned the depth of the sum of. The words were of agreement. A set of serious vows agreed to.

I felt a flow of electricity in my bones. I was excited but I also knew the responsibility.

She held my gaze.

'You are hers now.

'You are yours now.

'You are eternally accepted.

'You have made the vows and all will be as you have agreed.'

I felt on fire, yet calm.

I felt I was radiating heat and calm and power.

I felt at home. I felt relieved. I felt so much love.

And I wanted to share that.

Outwards, ever outwards.

Stacey Demarco

The whole [of their] term being completed, it was lawful for them to marry, and leaving the sacred order, to choose any conditions of life that pleased them; but of this permission few, as they say, made use; and in cases where they did so, it was observed that their change was not a happy one, but accompanied ever after with regret and melancholy; so that the greater number, from religious fears and scruples, forbore and continued to old age and death in the strict observance of a single life.

– PLUTARCH ON THE
VESTAL PRIESTESSES

Don't explain your philosophy. Embody it.

– EPICTETUS, STOIC PHILOSOPHER

CONTENTS

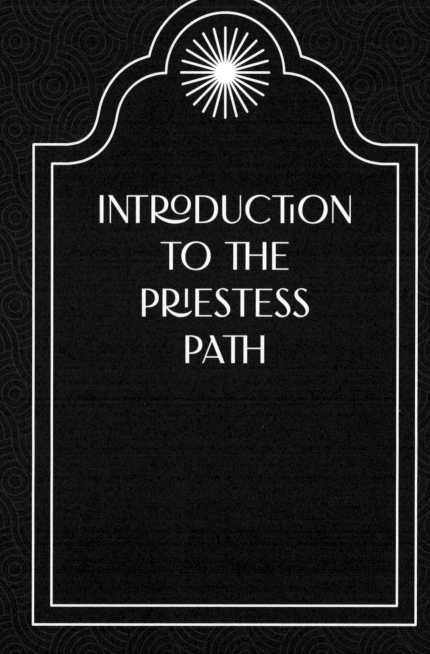

INTRODUCTION TO THE PRIESTESS PATH

WHAT IS A PRIESTESS?

I think the role of the priestess in both ancient and modern times can be misunderstood.

Most people would understand the modern role of a priest in today's culture because in the Christianised West we have come to easily acknowledge a masculine figure being the intermediary to the monotheistic traditions of religion.

Back in the ancient world, though, both feminine and masculine roles existed as conduits to the gods. In some traditions the priestess – a representative of the feminine in divine – was necessary to be the conduit to feminine deity. In some of the oldest continual cultures in the world there are times when there is secret women's business and the same for men, and these mysteries and places are not revealed to the other.

While we have some idea about the lives of priestesses from cultures that have limited recorded history, whether it be oral writing or in art, there is a huge swathe of the world in which while we know priestesses/ shamanesses/holy women existed, archaeological records sadly haven't captured much of their traditions. We can only guess at the mysteries and presume that in these cases we have some traditions that have been passed on to the practitioners of today.

What we do see in common is the idea of priestesses being leaders, catalysts and often healers or keepers of vital information. And so I will say that to me being a priestess, then and now, is centred around service to the community.

Serious service.

THE ROLE OF
A MODERN PRIESTESS

The age of the guru is over.

I say this not to be provocative but to simply state that the days of blindly following a guru – often a male – and giving your power and sovereignty away to them is both unnecessary and absolutely counterproductive.

The role of priestess or shaman is one of service, not of standing up on a stage being admired and having your feet kissed. In fact, historically they were the others often set slightly apart from their communities in some way because of their special role, relishing their solitude and otherness and not courting adulation.

This life of service is not a life of servitude; instead, it is a life quietly leading, honing your skills and passing on what works. It is not about external power, but power and strength built from the inside out. True priestesses do not seek others' approval, they seek to be a conduit of power in service. There is great humility in this and yet also a solid, quiet power that is unmatched. It is not a 'power over' but a 'joining with'.

A modern priestess embodies her philosophy and shares tools and skills to make the lives of those she serves better. If someone tells you they are a priestess ask them to tell you how that title came about, then you can decide whether or not they have earned that title. It's a jungle out there now. Observe.

For those of us who have been around a while we have certainly seen that there are spiritual fashions. It used to be angels then ascension or doing ceremony, and now strangely it seems folks are turning all pagan (and teaching it) when they are not. I feel it is dishonouring those who have

3

taken years to train and learn to be who they say they actually are. Do not give your power away in order to become empowered. It is always buyer beware, caveat emptor, and it is up to you, the seeker, to ask the questions to satisfy yourself.

It is important for me to seek authenticity and pass on knowledge in deeply practical ways and model what I know and what was granted the same way to me. That seems truthful.

To give people a certificate that says they are experts in being a witch or pagan or in the magic of the moon means they do not understand the very nature of what those things are and where they have come from. Who is the recognised authority? Where is the respect for these pathways? Is the learning not endless?

I have my share of formal pieces of paper in frames, but never will they be to prove who I am in the pagan or magical worlds. I'll let my actions tell that story loud and clear. I am not for everyone. Neither are you. However, I think by actively modelling to others what you say you are with ethics and service, with expertise and humility, you will reach those who need your leadership or assistance.

I have been researching, actively experiencing and teaching pagan spiritual paths for many decades now. My background is in business and professional writing so, just like many of you, I tried a rational way to find a path that would support me and enrich my life. I found teachers. Eventually good ones. My elders are a wonderfully mixed bunch of nationalities and beliefs. I travel extensively, not to sit by the pool in some resort but most often to immerse myself in a culture or way of life to learn in an open-hearted and respectful way.

Never with this attitude have I ever pushed to ingratiate myself with a teacher, ritual or way of being. It is my experience that true elders – not plastic shamans or gurus looking for their next pay cheque – are genuinely curious but watch you carefully and then choose to share with you . . . or maybe not. Learning from them takes time and you must be patient. It's been my experience too that I have learned by listening, watching how they live and by their example.

True teachers in this realm show you what you need, demonstrate it when you are ready and do not hold back knowledge for effect or money. You earn their trust and respect and the process is often very slow – or at least it feels that way to us. They may push you to greater heights and depths, but you don't become all seeing and all knowing because you did a few weekend trips or feel as though you can label yourself as a shaman/priestess/priest and so on. In fact, the label isn't even in your thoughts. The experience, however, is.

They are not your friends, they are your teachers; therefore, they may exhibit strong boundaries on their time or process but this is presented in an experiential way, not in a 'my way or the highway' method. Caveat here: unless there is a safety reason.

There is no one way.

Let me speak on this a little: if you find yourself furiously defending *your* way as *the* way, I would question why. I think robust discussion is healthy. This is one way we learn, but to shut down others who think differently is clear testimony to me that you are deeply unsure. If someone says they know their way is *the* way, run. Run, Forrest, run. In the path of the priestess this absolutism leaves no room for growth.

I remember returning from Bhutan, one of the most devout and authentically spiritual places I have ever visited. The beliefs are woven through every aspect of life, from ecology to government to sport. As a pagan in a strongly Buddhist country, the similarities between my beliefs and theirs was immediately noted, not the differences. My habit of picking up rubbish on a hike was seen and passed on to a monk we met. He gave me a card with a picture of the deity of the forest with a blessing saying that the deity had seen my valuable work. Good to know!

As I walked, the discussions with lamas both great and small, in famous temples and the most highly remote were friendly and joyful. After asking whether I was Buddhist (I'm not), they all quickly sought out information about the tenets of what I did believe and the harmony that could be found. So much learning. So much laughter. Such a warm welcome.

'Ooh! Who are you?' asked one monk. 'So many Westerners here in buses now but few make the climb to see us. Come, take my cat and share

chai and let's talk.' Recalling the curiosity and ease and that cat make me smile even writing this now.

When I came home I began to reconnect on Facebook and the contrast was incredible. People posting statuses about their beliefs but not willing to discuss why in even the slightest way. People ego tripping about what they are and who they have trained with. People collecting Facebook friends to market to. People competing for clients. People confusing religious terminology and giving them their own often-strange meanings. Friends having others try and steal their work or having people push in where they don't belong simply because of jealousy or fear of missing out – of what, I'm not sure. From where I stand right now I see very clearly the Western view of what spirituality has become: all show, little depth.

Witches were always considered to be the wise ones of the village. They could be relied upon for healing and good counsel. Very few leaders in ancient times made major decisions without first consulting the wise of their country or those who were able to translate oracles. Oracles such as that at Delphi were famous for hundreds of years and gave guidance to kings and those who would be kings.

Our problem, of course, was to find ways to continue or evolve our traditions during the long periods of persecution in later times. Happily, attitudes have changed somewhat in that we aren't burned anymore and there is a noticeable resurgence in bringing back some of the old traditions and celebrations, particularly those that mark significant moments in our personal timeline such as cronings and birthings. For example, we are seeing the original pathways officially re-recognised in places such as Greece and new pagan temples built in Iceland.

I see this as a positive step and as such we need more leaders, those with good foundational training to undertake such roles. We need those who build inner strength from the inside out, which often makes them immune from the need to people please, to abuse and to seek more and more power.

SERVICE, NOT SERVITUDE

I hear a lot about how tired folks are, particularly women. In nearly every Western country in the world women are still the primary caregivers of children and do the most domestic work within the home, even if they also have a job outside the home. In my home country of Australia the statistics, according to the latest Household, Income and Labour Dynamics Survey, looks like this: women are doing approximately 21 hours a week more than men in these unpaid tasks.

Additionally, the higher paid a woman is compared to her husband the more home chores she actually does! Yes, reread that. That unequal distribution of domestic labour falls into a pattern documented in a recent analysis published in the journal *Work, Employment and Society*. New mothers take on more housework than their husbands – and even more so when the woman makes more money than him, according to the article by Joanna Syrda, a professor at the UK-based University of Bath School of Management. 'We see these top female earners as compensating in doing more housework,' Syrda said, 'not when women out-earn their husbands but when mothers out-earn fathers. So, parenthood seems to have that traditionalising effect.'

Syrda's study used research from the Institute of Family Studies and examined the relationship between spousal income and the division of housework from more than 6,000 dual-income, heterosexual married couples between 1999 and 2017. Women with children reduced housework from 18 to 14 hours a week as they went from earning zero to half of the household income, but the analysis found that after passing her husband's salary a woman's home tasks increased to nearly 16 hours a week. In contrast, a man's housework ranged from six to eight hours a week when he was the primary breadwinner but then declined as his wife out-earned him.

Wow! That is some kind of compensation women feel they have to make.

Hours are long for everyone, though. For many people mortgages are huge, debt looms large and worries are big. The lines are blurred between work and home with our devices being on and we become more available to all almost 24/7.

Then there is this seemingly worldwide epidemic of insomnia. While most people will at some stage have a sleepless night, more and more people have problems with not sleeping well or sleep being interrupted. There are obviously serious medical issues with not getting enough sleep, ranging from lack of concentration, eating disorders, unwanted weight gain, high blood pressure, increased possibility of heart attack, depression and decrease in fertility. So, naturally, sometimes when I suggest to Priestess Path students that being a priestess is primarily about service I can tell not everyone is taken with that idea.

They might say: 'I'm exhausted, Stacey, I have so much to do and now you are asking me to do more for everyone else?' or 'I want to help others, but service? I've had enough of that,' or even 'I already feel like a servant, I don't want to be ground down anymore.'

I hear you, but there is a difference between being of service and offering service – especially in a sacred way – and being a servant.

Now there is a lot of fashionable discussion out there about leaders being servants as a good thing, that putting people first all the time is the way to go. Personally, I think this is unbalanced and impossible to do in the long term without burnout. To give and give and give is unbalanced. It leads to resentment or a hardening of compassion even in the saintliest of people. Instead, I prefer the term sacred service and the idea of doing this for the common good.

What is the common good? Well, I love what the Stoic philosopher and one-time emperor of Rome Marcus Aurelius had to say in his wonderful journal *Meditations*. Marcus mentioned the term 'common good' tens of times in this text. In fact, he said: 'The fruit of this life is a good character and acts for the common good.' This means when we work on our own virtue or goodness we can work with others well and cooperate to form a better and more harmonious society. The foundation, though, starts with us, and we extend ourselves in service for reasons of growing goodness rather than ego or some kind of twisted people-pleasing style of belonging.

When you dedicate to the witchcraft path it isn't just so you can do spells and look cool wearing a pentagram. Yes, folks love the aesthetic, but the reality is much deeper than what it all looks like. You become a weaver of the worlds, a catalyst for change, a link with all that came before and all that will come after. Above all, you dedicate to being of ethical service.

We can indeed find a balance between the expression of our firm foundation and power with the role of priestess in service. Giving of ourselves in service means we want to serve with clarity about why and how.

There is no cloud of enmeshment in people pleasing, guilt or a feeling of resentfulness about what indeed we may get in return. We are in full control of what we give.

If we possess a strong foundation of personal power and are motivated towards the goal of sacred service then the burden is not a burden at all, but one of the key reasons we decide to lead and live.

WHY WORK THE 13 LESSONS OF THE PRIESTESS PATH?

* You can expect to be transformed by this pathway if you choose to be dedicated to the work.
* You will build your strength and power from the inside out.
* You can expect a sense of capability, sureness, flowfulness, courage, discipline and confident expansion. Things that used to bother you will not be on your radar anymore.
* You'll be able to handle difficult situations with greater ease and with a solutions-based attitude.
* You'll be less fearful about making mistakes and understand that failure is simply a step in success.
* You won't be so scared.
* You'll see and break old patterns that prevent you from being powerful.
* You might just let go of who you were and be who you are.
* You'll be of service to something greater than yourself, and by doing so change the world.

WHY THE PRIESTESS PATH?

I felt a while ago that the time had come for me to offer some guidance based partially on traditional priestess teachings to everyone who was interested and for those who felt they were ready and could benefit from it. I felt, too, that it didn't matter so much whether people used the labels of 'pagan' or 'witch' or any other spiritual descriptor as long as they could understand the framework and be willing to actually take action.

You do not have to be pagan or a witch or even interested in these paths to benefit from these teachings. The Priestess Path is a year-long teaching of 13 lessons that will also weave and work with the eight major festivals of the wheel of the year as an energetic guide. The principles of stillness and growth and the power keys of self-knowledge, self-love, self-trust, self-care and leadership and more will all be examined and taught through the filter of the priestess.

We will delve into the idea of mysteries. Not knowing, but exploring and doing. Observing. Thinking big. The greater good. All through the processes we might use when training.

This book isn't a book giving a step-by-step guide on how to be a priestess.

Why wouldn't I write exactly that book?

Well, first, there isn't just one way, one tradition, one set of skills and ceremonies, and of course many aspects of magical initiatory pathways are indeed secret to outsiders. I wouldn't rightly be sharing the intimate secrets of the training I received over years, especially without physically being there with you. Second, not all of the priestess training is relevant outside the tradition or magical context it is formed in, yet some of it is and it can be common to many leadership pathways.

When I first decided to write this book I wanted to create a practical guide in which you had the opportunity to co-create as we went along. I wanted to make it simple and useful to you even if you simply dipped in and out rather than read it and practised for the entire year.

Therefore, allow me to explain some of the important aspects to note.

Pagans often have a more egalitarian view of the role of humanity in the world in that we do not see our human species as something outside of nature. We see us, just like all the other living things, as a part of nature, not apart from nature. This is a key distinction to make, and it is one often at the heart of those paths that fall under the pagan umbrella and many indigenous earth-honouring practices.

From this central belief a lot springs forth. A belief that we *are* nature. A joy in deep observation of the natural world. A deep and abiding respect for the way the earth works – cycles of all kinds can guide us. A curiosity and awe that flows through our interactions with the world every day.

Which leads to . . . connection rather than connectivity. An antidote to the fast and shallow and a satisfying answer to the yearning many people have for depth. A flowful yet disciplined way to frame your year. A powerful humility about human beings's place in the ecosystem but also the possibility for our greatness within it. And a feeling of care and responsibility for healing the damage we have done to the planet and to bring systems back into harmony.

For the purposes of this book I wanted to also have you consider one of the most well-known cyclic systems still used and, in fact, celebrated today. In the traditions of the ancient Celts and many parts of Britain, the year was broken up into eight seasonal festivals. These were festivals of earthly cycles, including the marking and celebration collectively referred to as the wheel of the year, and while you may not have heard of some of them – Lammas, for example – you would certainly have heard of Yule or the infamous Samhain, also known as Halloween.

I have included a guide to the wheel of the year in a section beginning on page 189. I suggest you mark or celebrate each celebration (I've included dates for both the northern and southern hemisphere) and try layering them over the work you are already doing. Simply start with the one that is coming up for you datewise when you start this book.

Each celebration has psychological themes that are calming and joyous for us to engage with. We experience in a real way the waxing and waning of light, dark, warmth, cold, fertility and fallowness, and of course life and death.

What I know for certain about following natural cycles closely like this is it is so rewarding over time. By honouring the cycles in these ancient but very deep ways we connect more deeply with being part of the whole. And besides that, the celebrations are fun.

HOW TO WORK FLOWFULLY WITH THE 13 LESSONS

I have begun each lesson with mythos.

One of the great joys of my life is to tell, listen to and work with the mythos of the ancient and modern world. Any of you who have worked with me or even read or used my printed works know that there is almost always mythos present.

'Mythos' is a Greek concept that simply means 'a story with a truth'. It's not the modern idea of myth, which is 'a lie or untruth'. I find it is often a deep and profound way to better understand life or to learn a lesson to make it better.

I can tell you to trust yourself, but you'll remember that point much more deeply if I tell you through the story of Rhiannon and the horses. I can express to you how important it is as a woman to have a sense of sovereignty, but if I tell you about Pomona you'll get it more deeply. I can tell you to think differently about fear through Ah Puch, to use your rational mind through Athena and to let go of your traumatic past through Kali, and you'll remember the stories forever and so the teaching becomes a part of you.

With my love of mythos came associations and friendships with people who had mythos to tell and share. Often these are First Nations people or people who have a cultural heritage in which such stories are simply part of their landscape. As is culturally right, only stories that are allowed to be shared are shared. Of course, some of the stories are shared only and especially between members of that culture because this strengthens the bonds and spiritual framework of that culture. At all times we must respect cultural guidelines on this; we should never steal or appropriate stories. We should never pretend these mythos are ours alone and we are the owners, when naturally we are not. The appropriation of stories is one way colonisers showed violence over the colonised. Language was stolen and often outright prohibited, and this included the passing on of oral traditions of mythos.

Some stories are shared with trusted people who are not culturally part of that community, and these people are asked to hold those stories to themselves in trust. Some stories are for everyone to hear, happily and generously, and these often change with repeated telling.

Then there are the mythos that change slightly due to locality. If we follow some of the Polynesian mythos that start in Tahiti and sing across the waters to Hawaii and eventually through to New Zealand we experience similar deity names starring in similar stories with similar places featured – all similar but not quite the same. To me this is testimony of the power and strength of the Polynesian navigators spreading their traditions and lessons as they sailed great distances from island to island. The stories changed partially due to the landscape and the eventual language changed. What is correct telling in Tahiti perhaps sounds wrong in Hawaii . . . but, of course, it is not.

The thing that some folks don't understand is that mythos have morphed and changed over time and circumstance. Stories that started and were told began to be told differently when, for example, a conqueror came with a different view or certainly when a monotheistic religion came across them. It is very common for strong female deity or figures in mythos to be turned into a villain or even a horrendous monster of the story. Look into the changing role of Morgan le Fay in the Arthurian myths for a good example.

As most of you know I always suggest going to the original source when studying mythos but also to understand what was going on at the time for there to be an interpretation such as the one you are seeing. I also suggest people read mythos like this out loud or learn the story to be able to tell it accurately orally to someone. This is how most mythos was passed on in ancient times, and still is in places now. By doing this you'll see how powerful the desire or urge is to embellish it as your own, and you'll see how meaning can change simply by the way you perform it or what you include or omit. For example, telling the story of the hero Perseus killing Medusa is one thing, but to include how Medusa became a monster to start with changes the story somewhat.

I think it is important when working with mythos to understand that there can indeed be many versions of the same story, and to tell someone that the version of the mythos they tell is a mistake or they are wrong is sort of irrelevant. Don't get caught up in that. Instead, it is more useful to understand why the mythos may have had a change in expression and what was closer to a first telling.

The very nature of mythos is that it does morph, that it is indeed alive and is often meant to be used as a guide to behaviour – a guide to a certain truth – even now. Isn't it an amazing expression of humanity that we can learn from the wisdom of stories created millennia ago?

The next step in each teaching is walking the path, which is an explanation and exploration of the lesson itself. It should give you a clear idea about what the lesson is and what it can do for you.

The third step is a series of tasks. The answers to the tasks should be recorded in a journal or safe file on your device. Action should come from this thinking and recording, and it should take time to complete. It is the tasks that begin the action-oriented path of the priestess; you don't just get insights, you do something with them. Lessons are only really integrated through doing. I can't do them for you. Only you can do them for yourself.

Finally there are the magical workings. Even if you have no interest or experience with the goddesses or gods mentioned in the mythos, having a go at a working is powerful. There are rituals, meditations, spiritual skill-based exercises and ceremonies featured for you to try. To me they are the engine of the change this path brings, and they give you a taste of the kinds of woven alchemic magic priestesses are a conduit for.

We absorb and learn as we progress and this path is an experiential one, so please do try these workings. You'll notice the difference within yourself if you do.

HOW TO GET THE BEST OUT
OF THE PRIESTESS PATH

GIVE YOURSELF SPACE

Get yourself a nice journal or open up a special folder on your device; this will be your working book. This is an experiential guide, meaning you have to engage with it. This will also give you space to work things through and eventually a record of how you have grown.

Give yourself a quiet place to do your tasks. Give yourself space to process them. Many of us have skills to hold space for others, so offer this to yourself while you are working.

GIVE YOURSELF TIME

There are 13 lessons to be engaged with roughly for a year, or 13 moons. Yes, by all means read the book through once so you know what you are getting into, but *Priestess Path* is designed as an experiential practice. If one of the 13 lessons is proving to be challenging and you need more time, give yourself that time but do not stop the flow. We should walk through difficulty, not sit stagnant within it.

PRACTISE IS EVERYTHING

When I speak about developing a spiritual or pagan practice I speak about 'practise' as a verb, a doing word.

There comes a time when we are ready to become who we have always wanted to be.

There comes a time to be still, to centre ourselves and feel out what we really have inside of us.

There comes a time to build our resilience, our strength and our confidence as well as our capacity for joy, creativity and action.

There comes a time when we are ready to reject our reliance on the external for our pleasures and self-worth, for this is such false power.

There comes a time when we are ready to develop *real* power.

And the yearning is great. There are so many of us.

That time is now.

TEST YOURSELF

As you progress through this book you will change. You'll feel it, especially from the inside out. You'll feel steady and strong and you may even notice the chaos around you swirling although you are not a part of it.

We are in a time on this planet when we need more authentic and kindly powerful people who are ready to step up and model what living a life of clear intent is without being distracted by the external drama and manipulation.

Test your newfound power in small ways at first. Try something new, stand up for yourself, create a boundary, say 'Yes' to something you want but is challenging, raise some power for magic, focus on you if you don't usually – whatever it is, risk a little. See what happens. It's gonna be good.

I

BEGINNING WHERE YOU ARE

Humble beginnings; the pull of change; evolving from chaos; the firm foundation; don't look back too much, you aren't going that way; creativity; committing; initiating; steady she goes

THE MYTHOS

Gaia

Almost every culture has a creation myth and the ancient Greeks were no exception. It was understood that at first there was nothing but a primordial sludge, a full swirling nothingness, a place of possible power. This state was called 'chaos'.

Then there formed some organising influences that stepped from chaos, the first of which were Eros (love) and then Gaia (Earth).

Because love existed and wove through everything, Gaia gave self-birth to Ouranos – the sky, Ourea – and the mountains and the sea – Pontus. She considered Ouranos her equal and they became joined. Ouranos (Uranus) exploded in joy and love, showering her with stars and rain, and Gaia begot other gods, goddesses and titans. Although Gaia and Ouranos ended up separating, Gaia still went on creating on her own.

The earth goddess has been venerated in her role as creatrix since time began. Gaia is an extremely old energy. As humans, from prehistoric times to post modernism we have witnessed and been awed by the magic of creation, whether it be the growth of a plant to nourish us from a tiny seed or the miracle of the birth of a baby from the sexual act.

Gaia may well have been worshipped originally as the ultimate mother, the first energy to nourish and provide creative fertility. It is rational to suggest that the more fertile the land the more food and game to hunt; therefore, the more people survive. The masculine entity was developed as the hunter, the one who ruled animals and game. If pleasing or honouring the earth mother in simple or ritualised ways enabled the earth to offer more edible plants and medicine or encouraged conception, this seemed a rational way to ensure survival.

As an energy, Gaia is said to have celebrated and rejoiced in her creations whether they be plant, animal, wind, rain, sight, sound or titan. Even when her creations sometimes horrified her she still protected them and found a place for them. True creation always brings with it a spark of joy and pleasure that carries across the world.

The word 'Gaia' has become a popular one among modern spiritual people, and she is no longer just a goddess owned by the ancient Greeks. When people speak of the living spirit of the earth they often name it Gaia. We now know much more scientifically about the earth and the systems that make it work than our ancient Greek friends; however, the way they saw that Gaia was a living cycle with interconnecting influences does them much credit. Even the idea that there was a big bang of sorts out of the primordial chaos is something that our brightest scientists are only just getting their heads around, but was simple truth for the Greeks.

Gaia is the ultimate expression of creative power. When you need a creative spark to arise within you, when you are tired of doing things the same old way or when you need growth within yourself, turn to the deep, loving, creative energy of Gaia. If you are in a career that requires consistent creativity such as the arts, music or advertising, she is a wonderful deity to assist with keeping a steady flow. For those who are literally creating – mothers – and for those involved in environmental protection she is an invaluable ally.

Ta'aroa

Ta'aroa is the Tahitian god who created all things. In the beginning there was an empty nothingness and it was only he who existed, cocooned within a smooth white egg. Ta'aroa travelled through this space willing for more within his current existence. He cracked open his shell and found himself in a dark space of nothingness: no stars, no earth, no sound, no smells, just him.

He broke the shell completely and took the pieces to create the rocks and sand and soil, forming it into a ball. He curled over and his curved backbone formed the mighty mountains. His joyful tears pooled into lakes, rivers, rain and the ocean itself. With his own feathers he created the birds, and with his fingernails the scales on reptiles and fish and the shell of turtles. He allowed his blood to spill a little, and it formed rainbows in the sky. His breath formed the winds.

From the clay he fashioned and created other creators. To begin was the first god Tāne, then Hina, Ru, Māui, Lono and many, many others. All had their realms and were sovereign over them. Tāne hung the moon and created the sun and stars so there was a sky. The earth was then fully created and Ta'aroa decided to create the being of man. Man was created and quickly multiplied, delighting Ta'aroa.

There is a yearning for creation within man. Man begins to create too, raising himself from the clay and travelling through the levels of earth, being innovative, having ideas, creating over and over again.

· WALKING THE PATH ·

Like many pagan or earth-honouring people, being engaged with nature is part of my practice so I enjoy spending time walking through the landscape. Hiking and often camping as I go is something I have enjoyed for many decades; I have hiked with my husband or with groups in quite remote places – and sometimes not so remote. As a hiker I think it's pretty much universal to say that once in a while we all might take a misstep or wrong turn and find ourselves a bit off the track.

So when we feel that we have lost our path or when we are deciding which route to take it's important to stop and take stock of where we are before making the next move. Of course, this might mean switching on the GPS, which gives a super-accurate picture of where we are, or if doing it the old analogue way we can use a compass and map. We might climb a tree or find a bit of high ground to get a better view. Either way, knowing where we are and in what terrain enables us to make good, informed next steps.

When we begin something new and especially if it is something that *matters*, something that will flow through us with lasting change, it is worth turning on our internal GPS and pausing and acknowledging the place in life we find ourselves in right now. Knowing where we are, standing tall and with honesty and humility, knowing as much as we can about ourselves and our capabilities, acknowledging the place in life we find ourselves, knowing what we have achieved and taking stock.

A full and complete inventory of our life, as it is can be a powerful place to begin a new way forward. To really stop, take a breath and stand where we are in honesty. We can examine our strengths. See what is missing. See what we can do better. Work out what we need. We might also need to apologise to someone or make amends. We might have to step away from how things are or the company we keep to have the kind of life we most yearn for, but the bottom line is we need to start where we are.

We need a deep dive into what is because, honestly, what is can be a place of total possibility to create into. This is an inherently powerful

position. And we can see through both our creation mythos that this idea of creation – of yearning, building, transforming and eventually world building – comes from an often messy or chaotic state or one of yearning. For example, the beauty of the image of Ta'aroa inside his cosmic egg dreaming of more is profound.

We, too, can create from our own yearnings and higher thoughts should we listen and feel. We need to circle back and be sensitive to what messages are being sent. We need to also return to the importance of what is and our home of earth. Gaia eventually faded from the active worship of the Greeks in favour of other deities, sometimes those she actually bore. Over time humans forgot about the earth, and her delicate cycles and we began to worship the gods of industry with little thought to the impact on the earth.

Today we are well aware of the consequences of a growing human footprint and climate change. We wipe whole species from the earth, we destroy her very fabric through nuclear bombs, we mine her lifeblood, we rip out her trees from an already depleting soil and we influence the temperature with our pollution. Will we be able to halt our destructive natures rather than connect with our peaceful creative ones in time? Will we truly be able to connect with our original mother and balance again?

A pathway like that of the priestess requires us to look more deeply around our actions on earth and defend nature.

TASKS

1. Connect with the earth in a real way. Go outside and stand or sit directly on the earth. Place your attention on your feet or sit bones. Keep your eyes open and take three deep breaths. Close your eyes and take another three deep breaths. Again, place your awareness on your feet or sit bones. Feel your own stability, your own foundation as part of the earth.

Open your eyes when you wish. Repeat every day for seven days – or more!

2. Write down answers to the following:

* If I look back on my life so far, I know these things/actions have turned out well for me . . .
* If I look back on my life so far, I know these aspects of myself are strengths . . .
* Like every other human being, I make mistakes. What do I usually do when I make a mistake? How do I act?
* How does this work out for me?

3. How do you answer your creative yearnings? Remember that 'creative' doesn't have to mean an artistic endeavour; rather, see creativity as the act of creating and growing something.

· MAGICAL WORKINGS ·

Opening to Gaia

Go into a favourite place in nature, one that speaks to you of Gaia. Light a candle with intention. Begin to breathe slowly and deeply, gradually becoming aware of your relationship with the environment around you. As a woman you may like to take your breathing down through your belly into your womb. Imagine breathing in and out through this sacred place of creation.

Begin to open all your senses to Gaia, extending yourself and reaching out to her like roots would search through the soil.

First, your vision. Look around you, open your peripheral vision and look at the detail of her, from the tiniest insect to the expanse of the sky. Soak in what you see and give thanks to Gaia.

Go to your aural sense. Close your eyes and concentrate on the sounds around you. Listen closely to the layers of life. Be very still and listen to your heartbeat and the way it melts into her soundtrack. Again, give thanks to Gaia for her connection with you.

Continue this through your other senses: taste, touch and smell.

When you have connected completely in this way, stay in this very open state and allow any messages that Gaia has for you to be integrated into your body and mind. Feel the unfiltered pleasure that exists in your body when you open to your senses.

Thank Gaia. Slowly close your senses back to their usual level, or have them a little more open than usual if you like.

When you have connected completely this way it is time to make your promises to Gaia. Dedication isn't just words but deeds. Use your own words to dedicate to Gaia, but also back it up with what you will do as an individual to support Gaia as she does you. For example, someone I know, after dedication, spends one day a month working for the World Wildlife

Fund, another has become a keen organic gardener and another has become the recycling person at the office!

You may also choose to dedicate a talisman or piece of jewellery to Gaia to remind you and bind you to your promise.

Spell for creation with Ta'aroa

This is a beautiful and hopeful spell to do within nature if possible. A new moon phase is a great time to cast, but any moon is magical!

You'll need:

* a fresh egg
* textas
* a white or green candle
* flowers
* a place in the garden to dig a small hole or a pot with soil
* a small bowl of aqua luna (water left out under a full moon for blessing).

Ahead of time, carefully take the egg and textas and write the things you most want to create for this year on the eggshell. You can write words or draw symbols; it's up to you.

Go to the place in your garden or outdoors you have chosen. Light the candle. Put a flower in your hair or behind one ear. Take a breath. Close your eyes if you like. Say:

> *Creator of all things, Ta'aroa, I humbly call you and ask you to help me create a year to remember for myself.*

Offer some flowers to Ta'aroa by placing them on the ground. Say:

27

> *As you created all things, allow me to break out of my current state and create anew.*

Crack open the egg in the hole in the ground or the soil in the pot. Imagine the growth and momentum beginning now towards everything you have asked for.

Cover up the egg with the soil. Pour a little of the aqua luna on the soil where the egg lays. Say:

> *It is here that it begins.*

Blow out the candle with thanks. Take action towards your creative goals.

Meditation in the field of possibility

Imagine a field of land in front of you. The land is fallow. It has been let to rest. Nothing is growing there, but you are aware that the soil is rich and alive. The sun is shining down. There has been recent rain and the air smells sweet.

As you observe the field you allow yourself to understand that this field holds infinite possibility. It is waiting for seeds to be planted, for life to begin in a bigger way. You allow yourself to imagine that right now this isn't an empty place or a void of nothingness, but instead this place is ready.

Just like you.

You now walk the field, removing anything that might hamper the growth that you intend. If there are stones or weeds, remove them. Remove any obstacles you find.

Imagine now that you are gathering seeds for the field. We aren't planting yet, but know what you plant here is yearning to grow. What do you intend to plant? What do you intend to grow? More peace? More joy? Creativity? Better relationships? A better business? A love of self? Take your time to

28

see those things that you wish to plant. Allow the positive and anticipatory feelings to rise. Feel good!

When you are ready you can come back to where you are right now. Know, though, that you can return and plant your seeds here in this field of possibility whenever you wish.

II

KNOW THYSELF

Gnothi Theron; the most famous oracle in the ancient world; the Delphic maxims; authenticity; who are we really?; warts and all; the holy boundary of the self; finding our real home

THE MYTHOS

Delphi and Apollo

The father of the Greek Gods, Zeus, fell in love with the nymph Leto, changed himself into a swan and seduced her. She became pregnant. Hera, Zeus's wife, naturally wasn't happy about this and sent a serpent, the python, to chase Leto across the world. Hera cursed anyone who supported Leto and stated that no firm ground would accept Leto in her labour. Hera felt this would make sure there was nowhere safe for Leto to go to bear the child.

Happily, the island of Delos, which was considered to be a land that moved freely untethered upon the ocean, accepted Leto and she was able to give birth to two babies, not just one. The goddess of the hunt, Artemis, was born first and assisted her mother to bring her twin, Apollo, into the world. Both twins shoot arrows that can bring favour or death.

Years went by.

Apollo hadn't forgotten about the horrible torment his mother had endured from the python. He learned that the python was a monstrous dragon/serpent sent by Hera to guard the sacred oracle of Delphoi (Delphi). It is suggested that the serpent was formed by the rotting slime left behind by the great deluge. Apollo laid claim to the shrine and slew the python with a volley of 100 arrows.

Apollo wanted the place to be a temple of light and learning so that all who visited would be able to know more and be more. Delphi became a shining beacon of healing and knowledge and was the home of the ancient world's most famous oracle, where his guidance was directly spoken by his priestess.

Pele

The goddess Pele was borne from the great earth goddess Haumea and the sky god Wākea in the ancient land of La hiki. She grew into a passionate and beautiful young woman who wished to see more of the world. Her parents were sad about their daughter wanting to leave but knew it was part of life to look for your own way and place, and all the family came together to help Pele.

Her uncle, Lonomakua, gave her the *pa'oa* or digging stick. The digging stick would enable Pele to dig into the earth for fire and create a home for herself. Her father sent a favourable wind, her mother supplied her with food and, in the form of the great smiling shark Kāmohoali'i, sent currents that would swiftly guide his sister's boat.

Pele gathered her things into a red-sailed canoe, and as she had the responsibility of looking after her younger sister Hi'iaka, her sister came too but in the form of an egg that Pele held under her cloak. Pele arrived at the first of the northern Hawaiian Islands and saw that this was beautiful. She dug into the earth with her pa'oa and fire sprang up, but only briefly. Water flooded the hole and made it a lake. No, she thought, this was not the place for me, so she and her sister sailed on.

Every island they encountered they stopped and Pele dug, but every time the fire would go out or water would fill the hole. She became a bit worried and doubtful but kept sailing. Pele finally sailed to the big island and found the mountain of Mauna Loa, and she began to dig. The fire was great and powerful, and the soil turned to ashes and formed Kīlauea. No water entered the hole, and instead red, glowing, liquid fire flowed.

Ah! '*This* is my home,' thought Pele.

Her brothers Kane-hekili (spirit of thunder) and Ka-poho-i-kahi-ola (spirit of the fire rain) joined her. Then, in the rich green forest surrounding Kīlauea, her sister Hi'iaka hatched from her egg. It was perfect for Pele, and this was where she made her home and became sovereign of the place of fire.

· WALKING THE PATH ·

In his role of sun god and light giver the shining Apollo was seen as the god of prophesy and oracles. The word 'oracle' means to 'speak through', and sometimes the oracles have indeed been living creatures, often people. In these cases the gods are said to speak through a person and the message may be directly interpreted by the receiver or through a priest or priestess. The most famous oracle in this form was that of Delphi in Ancient Greece, and Apollo was said to speak through the Delphic oracle, a priestess referred to as the Pythia.

The Delphic oracle would answer questions posed to her, and normally the answers would be in riddles, verses or in an unknown language. These would then be interpreted by the priest or priestess serving the oracle; however, the final decision on true meaning was always left to the person asking the question. This encouraged their inner intuition and wisdom to come into play.

The Delphic oracle was consulted by some of the most famous generals and conquerors of the ancient world including Caesar, Phillip, Alexander the Great and Croesus of Lydia, such was its power and political influence for over 1,000 years. The priestess sat upon a tri-legged stool on a rock and breathed in the vapours that rose mysteriously from a fissure near a sacred spring. This beautiful yet somewhat harsh place was considered the closest place to Apollo on earth and was the *omphalos* (navel) of the known universe. You can visit Delphi today if you visit Greece. It is still a very energetically powerful place with amazing ruins and a wonderful museum.

At Delphi you could also find education and guidance. The Delphic maxims were a collection of 147 foundational statements that provided a framework for life of an honest and, it was said, virtuous way of living. These maxims were carved along the pilgrimage pathways. The most famous of the Delphic maxims, 'Know thyself', was one of the first three maxims carved above the entrance to the Temple of Apollo at Delphi in the sixth century BCE. It is still an instruction that makes absolute sense for modern life.

To know ourselves is lifelong work, yet to begin to turn inwards and realise this is something we all need to do to make the most of life is work for now. The ancients knew that by knowing ourselves well we could build on our strengths, reduce negative patterns, transform our shadows and, by default, build empathy for others.

To know ourselves well means we understand the nature of what I call the 'holy boundary of the self'. This is the boundary that surrounds who we really are in our strengths, weaknesses and light and shadow. To know this, where this is, what this is deeply, means that we know when to say 'No' and 'Yes' and we develop a powerful sense of wisdom, self-trust and groundedness.

Sometimes, though, we don't trust ourselves. We come to think that all the answers to our problems are outside ourselves and we consult lots of other people for advice. Remember that even though we can gain good advice from others, the foundation begins with ourselves. Knowing thyself means we can generate the first steps of power from the inside out. Our inner power starts here.

Apollo asks us to look for the rational truth in the situation, including within ourselves. Ask and your questions will be answered. Find balance. Know thyself – take the time to uncover and connect with who you really are and what you really want.

We see clearly in this mythos that the goddess Pele knew herself. It would have been easy for her to stop her long and frustrating journey and settle for a place as her home that wasn't quite her. All that watery energy wasn't for her because she was fire, and knowing herself as she did she eventually found the perfect home for her with lava and fire on Kīlauea.

Pele is the perfect goddess to call upon when you feel directionless or unclear. If you feel bored a lot or unexcited about life it is her dynamism that you may need again. She is a creative force dedicated to moving you forward towards living your true purpose.

If you don't know what you want to do when you leave school or which course to take, or you are feeling a little stuck about what your next steps should be in life Pele will shake you out of your rut and get you moving in the right direction.

If you visit the big island and go to Hawai'i Volcanoes National Park you'll see the dancing red skirt of Pele as she rises out of the crater, a living goddess who creates the newest land on the planet through her glowing lava flows. She is what she is.

We are often tempted to people please or even fawn our way forward. Eventually, though, this reliance on how others will react to us is inevitably flawed. Leaving our own authenticity on the table and trying to be someone we aren't almost always ends with us in a weaker position, feeling resentful or lost. When we don't allow our true selves to shine through, when we live in the shadows of others' plans for us, how can we be truly powerful? Truly secure? Truly free?

TASKS

1. Is there an area in your life where being more rational than emotional may assist you?

2. Where would you like more clarity in your life and why?

3. Possibly the most famous Delphic maxim states 'Know thyself.' Do you know yourself? What have you come to know about yourself that has been the most useful?

4. Name your biggest strength and note how you developed this.

5. Choose one or two Delphic maxims and practise them (there is a full list on pages 208–210). Feel free to comment on the ones you chose, why and whether they are challenging.

⋆ MAGICAL WORKINGS ⋆

Invocation to Apollo

This is a wonderful invocation to this powerful god of enquiry and light. You can either get your answers at the end from Apollo through simple meditation or use your oracle cards!

You'll need:

* ✳ your favourite music playing, or if you play an instrument even better
* ✳ a gold candle
* ✳ some incense
* ✳ a piece of paper with your question or issue upon it
* ✳ your oracle cards if you are using these for answers.

Start by putting on your music or playing your instrument. Listen to it for a bit and feel good! Light the candle and say:

> *Shining Apollo, far reaching archer*
> *God of music and healing*
> *Protector of all and the one who answers*
> *Speak and answer my enquiry.*

Light the incense. Hold the piece of paper in your hand that has your question upon it and read it aloud to Apollo. Close your eyes and simply breathe. Allow clarity to flood through your body and mind. Allow any messages from Apollo, any ideas, emotions or pictures in your mind, to form and write these down. Otherwise you can consult your oracle cards, knowing that Apollo will speak through them. Say:

> *Thank you, wise Apollo, I know the answer will be clear.*

Blow out the candle. Be grateful.

Invocation to Pele

Here is a powerful meditation to connect you with the purposeful and creative power of Pele. It's a great way to get clearer about what direction you should take next, to uncover your purpose or to simply feel the passionate and creative power of Pele.

You might want to dress in Madame Pele's favourite colour, which is red, for this meditation or look at her volcano in Hawaii on the internet beforehand for some visual inspiration.

You'll need:

* ✳ a flower
* ✳ a red candle.

Place the flower in your hair. Light the candle. Say:

> *Aloha! Aloha! Aloha!*
> *I call you thrice*
> *Pele-honua-mea*
> *Pele-honua-mea*
> *Pele-honua-mea*
> *Madame Pele, Tutu Pele Ma,*
> *You who births the land*
> *You who shapes the land*
> *You who destroys the land*
> *Visit with me now if it should please you.*

39

Shut your eyes. Breathe deeply and centre yourself. Imagine standing in front of a volcano. You are perfectly safe. Put your attention on your feet and feel the earth vibrating beneath them. Extend your energy down a little into that earth. Feel how warm it is, how alive. Smell the heat in the air and feel the warm wind rustle your hair. Hear the soft roar of the volcano.

Look now at the volcano. Look at the amazing fire within the crater: how beautiful it is. See the glowing lava slowly pouring from the crater. See it now cooling and transforming into new earth. See how, bit by bit, Pele creates in a very purposeful yet dynamic way.

Again, place your awareness on your feet and imagine pulling up that powerful purposeful energy of Madame Pele and the volcano. Give this energy a colour if you like or at least feel the vitality of the energy rise up your body right to the top of your head. Say:

> *E-Pele!*
> *Thank you, Madame Pele*
> *Pele-honua-mea*
> *For your passion and purpose!*
> *Make my purpose clear*
> *Give life to my purpose*
> *Shake me from my slumber.*

Now feel Pele's fire within you. Clap three times and say:

> *Yes! Yes! Yes!*

Thank Pele for her help.

III

THE ONLY TRUE POWER IS DEVELOPED FROM THE INSIDE OUT

*Inside out versus outside in; the willow;
self-knowledge; self-esteem; self-trust;
self-care; radical self-acceptance; speaking
to ourselves as we would to our best
friend; we are what we do; naturally it's
going to take some time to change*

THE MYTHOS

Rhiannon

There was once a young king who lived in a castle upon a great hill. He had just been newly crowned and therefore began to look for a queen. This was a necessary business, but the young king was certainly lonely and looking for a great love. He had his mother the queen regent, of course, who had birthed him and brought him up in the absence of his father, who had died years before.

So it was that the king was out riding one day and saw a woman who rode her huge white stallion as well – if not better – than him. Her horse flew across the fields and the woman's hair flowed long and wild behind her. He kicked on his horse, and after some time caught up with her. Her face was flushed, her smile bright and her words joyful. Their eyes met and they fell deeply in love. After a time the young king realised Rhiannon, for this was her name, was all he wanted in a queen: loving, loyal, gentle, wise and fair.

He asked her to marry him and she accepted with grace and a full understanding of the responsibilities that would rest on her as queen, responsibilities that would now be relieved from the queen regent. While it would be natural for the mother of the king to be pleased for her son, secretly she was not. She was vastly jealous of what she thought was a usurper and she resented her loss of power.

The whole kingdom rejoiced in the union and thousands of people lined the streets to see the happy couple, which only enraged the queen regent more yet she hid her rage and unhappiness behind a mask of helpfulness and royal duty.

Soon a baby was born, a beautiful, blue-eyed son with a birthmark like a star on his leg who seemed to be the best of both his parents. Rhiannon wanted to look after her baby herself, not leaving him to wet nurses and others. She kept her baby with her as she slept in her chambers.

One morning when Rhiannon awoke she found her baby was gone from her. In its stead was blood, so much blood. She screamed her horror. The first in the room was Rhiannon's servant and her mother-in-law, the queen regent. 'Look, she has killed her baby! I knew she wasn't to be trusted,' yelled the queen regent.

Rhiannon's eyes went huge and wide. 'No, that isn't possible. Someone has taken him!'

The queen regent replied, 'Who could have taken him? You were here with him alone as you are most nights. Oh, you have killed him in your sleep! Where did you put him?'

With all the noise and chaos, soon the king walked into Rhiannon's room and saw the grizzly scene. He cried, 'Are you hurt? Where is our son?'

'I don't know!' wept Rhiannon.

'She has killed him! She's had a bad dream and killed him or perhaps just killed him because of her nature,' screamed the queen regent.

'I would never kill my child. I know this.' said Rhiannon.

'Yet you have. Look at the blood on your hands,' indicated the queen regent.

Rhiannon raised her hands to her face to see the blood upon them. The king fell to his knees.

'Well, I don't know why I have this blood, I don't know anything! I . . .' stammered Rhiannon.

'Well, I do know. She is a murderer. Take her away,' demanded the queen regent.

What the king and Rhiannon didn't know was that their son had been kidnapped by the queen regent in the night. She had killed a chicken and used its blood to make the scene against Rhiannon. The son was safe but hidden. The queen regent decided she would raise him on her own to take over the throne.

THE ONLY TRUE POWER IS DEVELOPED FROM THE INSIDE OUT

Rhiannon went to trial. She was found guilty, and by then felt that perhaps she had committed the crime. Perhaps, yes, the blood was her son's. The king was still so in love with her he could not kill her. Instead, he sentenced her to a job that would bring huge shame to her every day. As the castle was up on a high hill, visitors would be given a horse to travel to the top. Rhiannon's sentence would be to take the place of one of those hard-working horses and carry people to the castle upon her back.

Every day she struggled with her guilt. Every day her story was related to some new visitor, and in her extreme shame she would carry them upon her back to the top alongside the horses, never raising her eyes. She then went and slept in the stables with the horses, curled up and crying.

This went on for a year until one day Rhiannon became gently aware of the importance of the work the horses did beside her. People couldn't get to the castle without them and they bore the work with strength and focus. At night, at the end of the day, she also realised the horses were set free and in that freedom they ran, played, loved and foraged, mindful in the moment. She decided that she, too, would follow their example, bearing the guests with strength and focus, and when the day was done she would begin to enjoy her freedom again and walk around the city and countryside.

It was on one of these evening walks that she saw the queen regent playing with a little boy in a lower courtyard of a farm. He was on a small pony. She looked at the child and thought the king must have remarried quickly, for there was his new child so much like the eyes of her child. The small boy lost his balance and fell a short way, not hurt, but still a little shocked. The queen regent checked him over for cuts, and as she did so the little boy's trouser leg was lifted and there was the birthmark in the shape of a star.

Everything was suddenly made clear to Rhiannon. This was her son and she had been tricked – yes, the queen regent had tricked her but, worse, she had tricked herself. Rhiannon was able to call the local people together to witness the boy and the mark, and the queen regent, after denying who the child was, had to finally admit that she had stolen him for the better of the kingdom. Happily, the king had not stopped loving Rhiannon and reinstated her as queen and banished his mother into exile.

Rhiannon never again doubted her own self. Their son grew strong and wise and was a man of the horses. Rhiannon never forgot the lessons of the horses who worked beside her, and from then on no horse was a beast of burden in their kingdom but instead a symbol of freedom.

Artemis

Zeus, although a god, had some mortal favourites. His daughter, Artemis the huntress, saved one of the favoured mortals from certain death and Zeus called forth his strong and capable daughter to reward her.

'Daughter, I wish to thank and reward you,' said Zeus. 'I wish to give you what women seem to want most: a good husband. Allow me to choose one that honours you and your status.'

Artemis, a young and independent goddess, looked at her father in shock. A reward was all well and good, but a marriage for her was no reward! Speaking with her father about her future for the first time, she was quite horrified by the idea that she would have to marry at all since she loved her wild life in the green places. Why would she wish to give up her freedom, her hounds, her need for space?

Recognising that her father may be angry with her for her admission, Artemis gathered her courage and begged Zeus to allow her to never marry but to remain a maiden free of the confines of a home and to live wildly in the forests with just animals for company. She also asked that she be allowed to wear a short chiton or tunic so she could be unhampered in her movement. Zeus was profoundly moved by his daughter's authentic and stark admissions and granted her this unusual wish.

THE ONLY TRUE POWER IS DEVELOPED FROM THE INSIDE OUT

As she was now a true goddess of animals and of primal places such as the forest, Artemis received the finest hounds from the god Pan, and these dogs were chosen for their unmatched abilities to bring down lions, catch the swiftest hares and mark the lair of stags. She was so delighted with this gift that she was happy to allow Pan to share some of the realm and play his sweet music, but never did Artemis marry or birth a child.

· WALKING THE PATH ·

Inside out versus outside in

This is a big and important lesson, so take your time understanding this section.

One of the symbols of a witch's way is that of the willow tree. The willow has become a sacred symbol of growing your magic and power in a strong foundational way. Here is why.

A willow seems to grow very slowly and unimpressively at first. You see a tiny stick poking out from the often-sandy shoreline. Willows, remember, are most often found near water courses such as running rivers, and the edges of such places are unstable and open to change. At first you see this skinny stick and you think, good luck, little willow, one good storm and you'll be done!

What you don't see is the effort and energy that has gone on under the surface. Willows have huge, spread-out root systems that grow horizontally as well as vertically. They really take time to build this stable root system to give the small trunk a solid foundation. Then and only then does the willow put the effort into producing a strong trunk. Once the trunk has thickened and is a stiff brace the aspect that everyone recognises a willow for, those flexible branches sweeping the ground, can grow.

We can model ourselves on this great tree. We take time building our personal foundation, building our self-esteem, self-trust and self-love through dedicated attention towards ourselves, and like the root system of the willow it enables us to weather the worst storms life has to throw at us, even in unstable situations.

Our trunk – our body and mind – grows strong and upright. It is so robust that if we tried to push it over we could not. The foundation helps keep it strong and supported and we engage with the world with growth and an aspect of the ever-higher good, then we prize our flexibility – just like the branches of the willow are able to move with the wind and not break and grow with a nimble aspect, so can we. No being stuck or stagnant for us, instead a flowful and elegant way of working and moving through difficulty.

This analogy of the willow is only one reminder in our pathway to build the foundation first. The role of the priestess and of witches requires a belief that power is built from the inside out rather than the outside in.

Imagine a spiral going outwards like a big circle of power from the inside of you. It starts from you and moves outward, not the other way around. Building internal power has always been a priority for us due to the fact that it could have been quite dangerous in the past to rely on getting our recognition or power externally. It just may not happen when there is so much bias against us.

Additionally, without a high level of physical, mental and spiritual strength spellcraft and making effective magic is almost impossible. In covens, where the priestess is the conduit to the power raised by the rest of the members, it is imperative that she have an incredibly solid personal foundation to be able to channel and control that power so it is directed accurately. As a solitary witch or certainly as a priestess, this ability to be a clean and strong conduit to power is equally as important.

We believe that without a strong personal power base or personal foundation nothing lasting and strong can be built. To build inner strength in this way allows us to grow outwards with confidence and an unshakeable belief in ourselves.

There are four key areas that I believe our pathway chooses to concentrate on in order to build internal power. Each is as important as the other in building a more connected, happier, resilient person of service. It is vital, to get the strongest synergy, that we be mindful of developing all and not just the ones that seem obvious to us. The four keys are:

* self-knowledge
* self-esteem
* self-care
* self-trust.

Self-knowledge: know thyself

See lesson II on this topic, but I also need to make a special mention here of knowing yourself well enough to feel like you are living your values and being on purpose. Your purpose could be defined several ways but could include:

* why you know you are here
* what your core competency or life theme is
* what excites you, makes your heart sing and makes you feel focused and on-purpose
* how you are of service to the whole of life.

If we are fuzzy about ourselves it is virtually impossible to connect with what it is we are here to do. It is my experience that the familiar nagging feeling of something missing is usually a symptom of not knowing who we are enough to flush out our purpose – and live it!

The consequences of not knowing our purpose can most easily be seen when it comes to career and business. I think we would all know of someone who has had a midlife crisis in their 20s and 30s well before the old norm of the late 40s. There are more and more of us who wake up one morning, look at the jobs we have created for ourselves, look at our belief that we need more and more stuff to be happy, see our reliance on the connections of social media and look at our externally full but internally barren lives, and in utter shock recoil at our own choices. These uninformed choices are often a direct result of an uncovered, unlived purpose and this affects the way we react, respond, attract and connect with other people. Our relationships become at best satisfying but strangely restless and, at worst, totally destructive or co-dependant.

As an ambitious young woman I worked – successfully, mind you – in the corporate world. I was, however, living an unauthentic life by ignoring the yearnings of purpose and taking jobs one after another each for more money and to gain external power, which left me spiritually bankrupt. It wasn't until I began to dare to dig and uncover what was under the layers of insecurity, fear and this strange and kind of twisted people pleasing that I began to rediscover what it was I was here to do. What I didn't really talk about, though, was the cost of burying my true self in almost all aspects of my life, in particular for me within personal relationships.

Like many women of my generation I wanted more than my parents had. I worked hard for my education and had more opportunities and wasn't going to let that go to waste. The thing was, though, that no matter how focused I was on my own life or the life I thought I wanted, as soon as I picked a man my focus, sooner rather than later, ended up on him.

Why? The big answer is because I didn't know myself or trust myself. I would concentrate on and actively build up the businesses, careers and even lives of these men rather than my own. Anything other than to look at myself and my life. To do this and maybe find that void was terrifying. The smaller answer is that I was avoiding uncovering my purpose, because it seemed so unreal and unattainable it was easier to concentrate on helping someone else get theirs.

Unlike Artemis, I chose to place my attention on someone else rather than what made my heart sing and what really mattered to me. This also extended to problem-solving behaviour and being a white knight; for instance, saving partners particularly if they had addictions of any sort or motivation or money problems. I would come to understand that some of the actions I took were the classic traits of co-dependence, because not knowing myself, not trusting myself, meant I would do whatever I could to not be abandoned by someone else.

Let me also state that I totally take responsibility for my actions. These things didn't just happen to me. I also was extremely uneducated about this kind of thing. I chose the manner of my suffering. I consciously chose this behaviour because it was a survival mechanism and I knew no better, but let me tell you that the costs of this, although not immediately obvious at the time, were huge.

By negating my own life and purpose I got into debt, my relationships broke down, I felt empty, I felt lonely, unfulfilled, angry and resentful when I didn't get appropriate gratitude and got to live with the roller coaster of the mood swings of partners who had addictions and other demons. I let go of real friendships and made ones that were based on what status I could offer due to my area of work rather than who I was, and I would come back for more, one relationship with greater destructive power than the next.

It took some extremely hard consequences for me to stop people pleasing. By hard consequences I mean I could have literally lost my life. I was placed firmly on my arse with money. I got shamed and embarrassed. I feared for my safety. I felt stupid that at one point I got scammed by someone who I just couldn't quite believe was actually doing it because I had helped them in good faith. I had my suspicions, yet I didn't do anything.

This is where doing your own work enables you to see your part in things and not end up resentful or damaged. I now know my triggers. I know if I feel a certain set of emotions around someone I need to be mindful and check myself. I also know to ask permission to assist or to wait for someone to ask for help. I know to take all relationships slowly.

Does that sometimes look to others like I don't care? Perhaps, but these are often the kind of people who want someone to save them or take responsibility for them or who simply enjoy having someone dance around them. That is no longer me. They'll move on.

We must understand that the holy boundary of the self matters and that we can never trade our values, our strengths, our very authenticity for scraps at someone else's very wonky table.

A girlfriend and I were talking about these good ol' times one night. A former great white knight like me, she laughed and said to me that if we both had put as much blood, sweat, tears and thinking time into our own lives as we did our past male partners we would probably be the prime minster of our countries or a billionaire by now!

And all that people pleasing energy I used to have? That huge amount of power? Where did I put that? Where did that go instead of being misplaced? It went into me. It went into my own development and recovery and creativity. Oh, how my life changed! Equal partner. Solid friendships.

More time for creative work and more success. Deeper spirituality. A profound sense of happiness and peace more often.

That brings the ability to provide service to others in a stronger and more authentic way. It enables me to extend my energy outwards radiating in a great circle. That circle begins with me.

Now that I have a deeper knowledge of myself, both my strengths and vulnerabilities, my shining lights and my blind shadows, I can make better, more-informed decisions about my life, including my relationships. At first, learning to do this felt clumsy and unnatural. For example, I remember when I was beginning to date again and asking myself a set of questions before I accepted a date such as: does this man need saving in any shape or form? Nope. Tick! Does this man seem to like his own life? Yep. Tick! Does this man have any addictions of any kind that he is not dealing with? No. Tick! Does he need me to complete him? No. Tick!

Then I would bite my tongue every time I was tempted to offer a piece of advice or help him with a proposal. If I discovered they had an addiction I would walk; no negotiation. If they needed saving or had narcissistic tendencies I would run, not just walk.

This, of course, is a balancing act. Real support is something you want to share with your partner, but not if it stops you fulfilling your purpose because you are only focusing on them. I worked with Artemis energy – authenticity and freedom – regularly to enable me stay connected yet revel in my selfhood. I also ensured that I continued to follow the four power keys: self-knowledge, self-esteem, self-care and self-trust, which gave me considerable impetus towards a healthy balance.

Now I do this instinctively in my unconscious competence. Needless to say there is a lot less pain in my relationships and not just the love relationships. I know that not everyone will love me or even like me, and this is totally natural, yet the ones who do can do so because they know who I am and what I am because I do not hide it from them. They can engage with me all the more honestly.

Remember that the cultivation of self-knowledge and knowing yourself means that you'll want to start living in an honest way that reflects that.

This will mean not everyone will like you. You will have to release this idea – and it's actually an impossible idea – in order to thrive. Understanding that you cannot be everyone's cup of tea is a healthy belief to have. It's integral to your focus, healing and growth as a person and priestess.

Self-knowledge begins by asking and answering both the easy and the hard questions. Take a look at this lesson's tasks below for starters. If you can answer these kinds of questions clearly, keep delving as you evolve and progress. Participation and movement are the rewards of superior self-knowledge.

Self-esteem

Witches believe that we each have a spark of the goddess and god within us. In natural return the goddess and god have a spark of us within them. Knowing intimately that by having a spark of divinity within us we are indeed a goddess or god tends to change reality for us. It is difficult to experience self-hate if you know that you have the divine within you. Self-esteem comes flowing back, flooding us with positive change, if we come to this realisation.

Having solid levels of self-esteem is considered by psychologists as one of the keys to building successful and resilient relationships and generally having a balanced life. It is an area of psychology with the largest amount of research, and we have large amounts of data that shows that children at much younger ages are more aware of themselves, their bodies and their intelligence and how this compares against others of the same age and by societal standards. We know just how this affects their self-belief and behaviours; for example, many children as young as kindergarten age begin to exhibit negative changes in behaviour such as becoming more withdrawn if they believe they aren't as attractive as their peers. The story ramps up another level by the time children with low levels of self-esteem hit puberty. If self-esteem is not experienced or learned these young people have a higher than normal incidence of addiction, truant behaviour, health problems, self-isolation and unplanned pregnancy.

Adults who experience chronic self-esteem problems experience lack of resilience and poor societal, educational and career development, all of which are factors in experiencing satisfying personal relationships. Women in particular develop eating and body disorders that impact many areas of life.

The good news is that self-esteem can be developed even if we have missed out during our earlier development. The sources of poor self-esteem should be identified and, of course, self-compassion developed. Imagine if we spoke to our best friend the way we often speak to ourselves. Imagine telling our beloved friend that they were ugly or hopeless or stupid, or that no one would ever love them. No, we wouldn't, yet we do that to ourselves. We must identify and honour our individual gifts, bodies, minds and spirits. Knowing that your uniqueness, your differences and even the parts of yourself you consider unworthy can be the very things that make you powerful and special in this big wide world.

Examining the root causes of our low self-esteem with appropriate support can lead to an understanding that we, in fact, have adapted to dysfunctional situations, and sometimes it is someone's own trauma and disfunction that is thrown on you. Although knowing the causes doesn't mean that we automatically free ourselves of them, it's a start.

Self-care

It is truly a difficult job to write a section on self-care without sounding like a worried mother, but bear with me. I'll try not to take your hand and look deep into your eyes and tell you that you aren't looking after yourself enough. Some simple questions you may like to ask yourself around the issue of self-care are:

* Do I experience enough genuine moments of pleasure in my week?
* Do I feel vital?
* Do I regularly put work ahead of sleep, eating, family and pleasure?

* Does my body get enough movement?
* Do I have a close relationship or partner who I know will support me unconditionally in times of crisis?
* Am I over- or underweight?
* Do I consider times of play as important as times of work?
* Do I get prompt and professional assistance, be it medical, psychological or spiritual, if I require it?
* Do I consistently put the needs of others ahead of my own?
* Do I find it hard to say 'No' to requests that I really don't want to do?
* Do I find it hard to say 'Yes' to activities that I think would be great but feel like guilty activities?
* Do I believe or have faith in something bigger than myself?

An easy way to introduce the concept of self-care into your life is to simply ask upon waking and just prior to sleeping: 'What is it that I need to care for myself more?' or 'How can I be a better friend to myself right now?', or perhaps you could ask 'Please tell me what is best for me right now' and listen. These will be very short answers; don't allow yourself to think about this for long or edit the reply. They are short, sharp messages from the subconscious. Record the answer each night in your journal and, of course, act on them.

Here is a random sample of answers for me over the course of a week:

* go to bed early
* organise a dinner with friends
* disco Friday
* see the accountant
* bath tonight
* workshop August, not June.

An innocuous list on first look, isn't it? With a little explanation you will see how much this small communication improved my self-care during that time:

THE ONLY TRUE POWER IS DEVELOPED FROM THE INSIDE OUT

* I have a lot to do, and I have more energy if I go to sleep early and rise early.

* This will be fun and I would like to catch up with my friends, who are energising to me.

* Disco Friday means I knock off work a bit early and play 70s disco songs in my office. The only reason I do this is because I find the whole thing a bit absurd and funny. Listening and dancing to the Bee Gees or Donna Summer at the end of the work week is decompressing and fun.

* Seeing the accountant meant that I could stop doing the head miles about my tax.

* Bath tonight is always a certain relaxer for me and enables me to think creatively at the same time.

* Workshop August, not June, as I had been stressing that I would not be able to organise a June workshop as planned due to other commitments that had arisen. Reluctantly, I moved the date, although this was a great move as it gave me more time to prepare and less stress and more participants were attracted.

The best times to exercise radical self-care are when you are under extreme pressure. In order to be at your best, knowing what you tend to let fall away in times of stress can be the canary in the coal mine; for instance, nourishing food, clear communication with friends and family or adequate sleep. Establishing a clear plan of extreme self-care prior to times of pressure and you – and often those close to you – will have a better chance of getting through this more demanding time in better shape.

I'm going to especially mention our bodies and getting sick here. It is very tempting when things go wrong with our bodies to dislike or hate them. At the very least, many of us regularly get angry or frustrated with our bodies. I'm guilty of this, especially the frustration bit. 'Bloody ankle – another sprain!' I might say. 'Why play up now? I have things to do!' or 'Why don't you just work for me without pain?' or 'What now? Yet again, my stupid body has failed me! I hate you!'

While we are more than our bodies and more than our minds they *are* parts of us, and it all works in synergy. After all, your ankle is connected to other parts of your body, inflammation goes through all of your body and pain affects your mood and enjoyment of life; therefore, if you hate your ankle or knees or the bit that doesn't work so well you are hating yourself. It's logical.

While it is human to be unhappy about this kind of thing, keep it as a flash thought or train yourself not to do it so often. What has worked for me is to think this part of me is suffering and it's doing the best it can for me right now. Don't forget normal cells are actually programmed to do their best for you; that's scientific fact. Imagine instead that you think 'I have to lovingly support this part of me just as if it was a distressed puppy or baby. I would never ever yell at a puppy or a baby. I should be compassionate with myself.'

I found the absence of frustration and anger gave me some clarity and enabled me to find better ways to support my body. I no longer hate bits of my body simply because I don't want to hate myself anymore, and while having a pity party for myself might be okay for a short time, it ends up being no party at all.

Self-trust

I love to ride horses but as I learned to ride as an adult I don't possess the complete lack of fear the gorgeous children have at the stables I visit. There they are: literally tens of them, aged between five and 15 and confidently leading, galloping, jumping and manoeuvring animals that are literally half a tonne in weight.

I watched as one eight-year-old girl spoke to her friend as she faced a new jumping height on her mare Red. She examined the height intently as she led her horse to it. Both circled it like prey, and with a simple ease they trotted back up to the starting point where her friend was waiting.

'Yep, we can do this,' she said to her friend.

57

'Ooh, it's a bit higher than the last one. You better be careful,' her friend replied.

The girl smiled at her friend with shining eyes and said, 'Yes, it is higher, but I can lead Red to that and I don't need to think about being careful. Red does that.'

Off she went. Sailed over the jump like she had been doing it all her life. A huge smile and cuddle for her horse followed. As I watched I knew that I had witnessed the unerring power of self-trust rather than a lack of fear. I was reminded of the story of Rhiannon and the horses and how her lack of trust had caused her so much pain. No such self-doubt here!

Self-trust is a surety that we can rely upon ourselves. That our decisions are valid. That we ourselves matter. That knowing ourselves combined with trusting ourselves leads to better and more informed decisions about all aspects of our life. Witches and priestesses of our traditions believe that when we put our trust in ourselves, because we are connected with the goddess we put trust in her and vice versa.

Self-trust is far more than a flashy show of confidence. It is deeper and farther reaching than that. It is the security at the very core that, no matter what, my wisdom matters and it is best. It allows for flow and for faith in myself and the way I do things.

Self-trust is a full acceptance of self. As accepting oneself becomes easier, self-trust will begin to shine and this gives great momentum to anything we choose to tackle or do. Why not check your level of self-trust now? Choose to answer the following questions:

* Do I let my partner or family make all my important decisions for me?
* Do I believe what people say about me, negative and positive, without checking it with myself internally?
* Do I worry that someone will find out that I am not as good/loving/happy/sad/talented as they think I am?
* Do I worry that someone will find out that I am not perfect?
* Do I believe that I am not beautiful/good/talented enough because someone told me so?

* Do I fear confrontation or big challenges of any kind?
* Do I wait to hear what others have to say before expressing my opinion?

If you have answered 'Yes' to some of these questions, your self-trust could do with strengthening.

These foundational keys help us unlock our personal power, the kind of power we need in order to be priestesses and to be of solid service. Without this unshakeable core, any internal power we possess cannot cleanly radiate outward and obliterate obstacles by passing distractions, reducing fear and creating connection after connection. If we are constantly trying to glean all our power from sources external to ourselves we are reliant on what others are willing to give. Unfortunately, what they are willing to give may not be enough or what we need. Are you waiting for the crumbs off someone else's table?

Can a source of strong internal power be gained overnight? Nope. Can you build this unshakeable core from the inside out with practice over time? Absolutely.

In its simplest form, the formula for internal versus external power sources is:

Power built from the inside out:

Witches' keys to power x time + solid core self = power full

Power built from the outside in:

Lack of witches' keys to power x time = fragile core self = power less

---

It is an easy choice to be power full, but it is a choice.

TASKS

1. Take some time to journal answers to the following:

 ✳ Who do I believe myself to be?

 ✳ What do I really love?

 ✳ Do I experience what makes my heart sing?

 ✳ What are my strengths?

 ✳ What are my vulnerabilities?

 ✳ What do I fear?

 ✳ What am I attracted to?

 ✳ What do I value?

 ✳ Do I lack confidence in making new friends and relationships?

 ✳ Do I feel that I am somehow less than others and why exactly?

 ✳ Am I unhappy about who I am?

 ✳ Do I need to continually prove my worth to others including my family, friends and close, intimate partners?

 ✳ Do I automatically think learning something new will be difficult?

 ✳ Do I exhibit inappropriate emotions at times when I feel uncomfortable or lacking in confidence?

⋅ MAGICAL WORKINGS ⋅

Utisetta

The Norse had a tradition of sitting outside simply with the intention of experiencing nature deeply. They called this 'utisetta'. Sit outside, day or night, be comfy and warm with no phones or devices and just experience. Start by doing this for 15 minutes. Extend by an extra 10 minutes each week this month.

Invocation to Rhiannon

As Rhiannon is a moon goddess, a really good time to do this invocation for more self-trust is at a full moon phase. You might also like to dress in white or silver. If you are lucky enough to have a horse, groom it and carry some of its hair in your pocket. If you have a piece of jewellery with a horse charm, wear it. If you don't have access to a horse, print out a picture of one and pop that in your pocket.

Create a circle around yourself by dropping some flower petals or glitter around you in a circle, or if you go outside draw a chalk line around you or arrange some leaves in a circle.

Sit down with your back straight or choose to stand in the middle of your circle. Know that you are safe and loved within this space you have created. Know that Rhiannon on her horse is with you. Say:

Rhiannon
You were once like me
You doubted yourself
Fill me with self-trust
So mote it be!

THE ONLY TRUE POWER IS DEVELOPED FROM THE INSIDE OUT

Shut your eyes and imagine yourself being filled with trust in yourself. Breathe in deeply and imagine breathing in the power of self-trust. On the out breath, imagine breathing out any doubts or worries you may have. Repeat this several times until you feel very confident and that all your niggling worries and doubts have left you. Open your eyes. Feel how different you feel: more confident!

Thank Rhiannon, and know that as you step out of the sacred circle you have created you have more power than ever before to move out into the world in a more positive way.

IV

WE CAN'T ACTUALLY CONTROL ANYONE

(YEAH, I KNOW IT'S FRUSTRATING)

We only own ourselves; focusing on others;
people pleasing; the concept of sovereignty;
deflecting and procrastinating; what
happens if you place more attention on you?

THE MYTHOS

Artemis

Actaeon, the son of Aristaeus and Autonoë and a student of Chiron, was hunting with his friends and his famous pack of hounds through the forests near Mount Olympus. He prided himself on his hunting prowess and almost never returned home without game. He had boasted to his friends over cups of wine that he was the goddess Artemis's equal in his mastery and loved nothing more than to exercise what he was good at.

One day he became separated from his friends deep in the forest. He entered a thick grove of trees, and as he passed through he saw a reed-ringed pond of water. As he got a better view he realised there was a woman bathing in the pond and he quickly realised it was the goddess Artemis herself.

So beautiful she was! It occurred to him that in all propriety he should quickly turn away, but such was her beauty that he wanted to stay and see her even for just a few more seconds.

The goddess turned. She saw Actaeon and was outraged at his transgression of her mysteries; she would have no man see her and tell of it. She told Actaeon that if he tried to speak to anyone ever he would be transformed into a stag. Actaeon ran in fear away from Artemis. He was very frightened, but knew the rest of his hunting party must be near. He heard them calling for him, and without thinking answered them back and was instantly transformed into a great stag.

His well-trained dogs smelt the stag and begin to chase Actaeon. They cornered him against some great stones and he tried to call their names, but all that came out was a stag's bellow. He was killed by his own hunting dogs. The hunter had become the hunted.

Pomona

There was once a beautiful goddess called Pomona. She loved her garden above all else and felt more at home there than anywhere. From the first rays of the morning sun until the shadows ran dark at twilight she tended to each and every plant within her land. Her garden and orchard covered a vast area and her land was fenced so that no one could come in, so only she worked within it. Constantly in her hand was a silver pruning knife she used to tenderly curb too-wild growth or cut back wood that was dead and no longer of use to the plant.

Upon these plants Pomona lavished her attention and care. Every one of them was seen as an individual and as part of the whole. She watched for signs of dehydration or flooding and quickly adapted to the situation. No plant ever suffered from thirst and none were sick with excess moisture. No disease grasped the greenery, and when it was time for a plant to die it never rotted but was sewn back into mother earth, enriching the soil.

No tree was allowed to take the sun of another, so each grew steadily alone but was interconnected with the other plants and soil around it. Whenever a plant or vine did desperately or wildly go where it shouldn't, out would come Pomona's knife to guide it back to the best pathway. Thus, the fruits of her labour were succulent and lush. As she sat back on the soft grass at the end of the day and looked around she loved what she saw and felt within her soul.

Surrounding her was the richest and most actively growing garden on earth. In front of her the tomato vines were thick and coiled around every post, erupting in an explosion of colour and taste as the red fruits came to season. The orchard of apple trees to her left went on as far as the eye could see and each apple was a work of art inside and out. The nuts in the trees and bushes were rich and wholesome and the pear trees the sweetest in all the land.

So engrossed was she in her garden of delights that she did not feel the need for romantic company, and she lived and worked alone. Her gardens

65

were surrounded by fences lest the people of the village wander in and none of the masculine persuasion were welcome. This did not discourage those from trying to win her love. Gods, fawns and satyrs all tried to win her attention and her love but failed miserably. The goddess Venus may have been able to influence others, but not Pomona.

A god called Vertumnus was one of the many who watched her from outside her gate and fell deeply in love with her. No matter how he tried, winning her love seemed impossible. Vertumnus decided he would disguise himself in various forms he thought would be pleasing to her interests so he could learn more about her and seriously woo her. Through his shapeshifting he learned that she feared being coupled mainly because she thought she may need to leave her land and garden.

Vertumnus revealed himself and promised his love and that his own land would be joined to Pomona's, meaning a larger garden for her to be sovereign over and an even more plentiful garden if worked together!

• WALKING THE PATH •

You might ask what the story of Artemis cursing a peeping tom has to do with control. Even though Artemis was a goddess and actually gave Actaeon a chance not to look at her, she still couldn't avoid that he chose to. The bottom line is we cannot control others. In fact, we can't control most situations. We have no control over anything but ourselves. The Stoic philosophers of ancient Greece had this lesson as a core one. This possibly has had the most massive impact personally on my life.

We often think we have control over everything and we go crazy trying to control it all when this is actually an impossibility. You especially have no control over others. Really. Even kids and pets will get around you. When you stop worrying about the things you cannot control – including people – then you have more time and head space to focus on the stuff you can influence.

Read that again if you need to.

But what *is* in our control? While we can't always control the circumstances of our lives, how we react to these circumstances is in our control. Yes, we can get shocked by things, but after that initial, often default, reaction we get to choose. Yes, my friends, we indeed have a choice, a choice that should be a direct expression of who we are rather than who others would have us be. It should be a choice that exercises our free will and innate wisdom rather than our fear and doubt and drama.

You are better than that. Yes, you are.

We can get plenty of practice in this lesson. When you begin to rise in any real way, not everyone is going to be happy for you or like you at all. This idea was something that did not actually occur to me when I was younger. I did not suspect that people would be nasty to me purely because I had achieved something that didn't take anything away from them at all. Why would someone attack me or disparage me just because I worked hard to make something I wanted happen for myself?

It was a very wise friend who warned me just before my first book came out: 'This is a good book but get ready to get whacked. You raise your head above the line and you'll be a target.' I didn't quite get it then, but I soon did.

The book was published and people who were nice to my face were not elsewhere. There were lots of backhanded compliments. People would tell stories about me like they knew me when they had never met me. Even my partner at the time seemed to feel he had to compete with me. Therefore, I soon learned my wise friend was telling the truth and I had to decide what I was going to do about all of this. After all, I wasn't going to go back into my box, yet this was so hurtful. I wasn't going to be beaten back because the writing genie was out of the bottle.

The answer for me was to understand that the reaction of others to someone's rise, in this case my own, had nothing to do with me and everything to do with them. Their jealousy or discomfort was a pointer to what they wanted, and if they had used this for their own development – for example, jealousy is a pointer to what we want for ourselves – then some good could have come of this. At the end of the day I had to really integrate the truth that 'I am not in control of anyone else.'

Ever.

But I am in control of me, and what I can do and did is create personal boundaries that protect me and enhance my rise. Again I mention the holy boundary of self. This included observing but not involving myself in this sort of chaos, not exposing myself unnecessarily, having disciplined work schedules and surrounding myself with people who were genuinely delighted that I was getting success. As the Greeks say:

Be careful who you hunt with.

Being with people who cheer your rise is powerful, and giving them that gift in return is priceless. Go find those people if you aren't surrounded by them already.

All of you will at some stage I hope begin to rise. You'll be stepping up into something better, newer and more wonderful, into something you have long wanted or dreamed of. Equally, someone will be watching you do this and be uncomfortable for whatever reason and they will try and hurt you. I repeat: none of this has anything to do with you. You keep going and you keep rising.

If it's someone close to you and they are worth talking to in depth, have that honest conversation about what you are doing and what they are doing and try to come to an honest place where things can be worked through . . . but, friend, please *do no back into your little box.* That helps no one. I promise. The world needs your rise just like we all need the dawn.

Pomona reminds us that we do have control over our lives. We have unlimited plenty in our lives and the natural world that we need to cultivate and care for. In both a literal and figurative sense, there can be limited growth if we do not choose to prune back the dead wood in our lives.

For most of us there is always some aspects of our current experience that we would like to change. These things may take the form of an outmoded belief, bad habit, damaging pattern or plain and simple fear, or sadly a person who is afraid or jealous of our rise and tries to stop us. Often with these things we need to make a decision to finally leave them behind or cut them out of our lives once and for all. Just as Pomona holds her silver pruning knife ready, we too need to be ready to use our true wisdom and courage to free up our natural capacity for growth.

TASKS

1. A good way to get a feel for this is to think of a problem or an issue you have, get a piece of paper and draw a line down the middle. Head up one side with 'I have no control over . . .' and the other side with 'I have control over . . .' Break down the issue or problem only by these two categories. You will very quickly find that you were worrying about things you cannot control (ridiculous) and not focusing enough on the things you can control (also ridiculous). Leave the stuff you cannot control alone and instead focus your effort, to the best of your ability, on the stuff you can.

    Believe me, you'll have enough to do and what you'll do do will feel like a miracle in the way it moves you towards what you want. Again, focus only on what you have control over. If you are an overthinker or someone with anxiety, this one is for you.

⋅ MAGICAL WORKINGS ⋅

Invocation to Artemis

You'll need a stone or wood arrowhead for this; they are easy to make!

Decide on a walking or running route. Artemis loves the forest and the green so you might choose a park, bush walkway or even well-foliaged street. Also, think about what you want Artemis's help with and why you wish to invoke her. Ideal things to ask for are assistance with focus, being more independent, being seen the way you wish to be seen or running your own race in life. If you have a dog (your very own hound!) you may wish to take them along too. Artemis loves her dogs!

Hold the arrowhead in your hand. Begin to walk and say:

> *Artemis, of the wild places, allow me to walk with you in your green home.*

Breathe deeply and focus on the feeling of your body travelling through nature. Feel your muscles work and your body move. Also, be very aware of your surroundings: the birds, trees, sounds, temperature and smells.

Begin to accelerate your walk to a jog, or if you are just keeping it at a walk perhaps swing your arms a little more. Say:

> *Artemis, I invoke thee! I too move through the green. I ask for your assistance with greater focus and also with [insert your intention]. You who are a protector and a huntress who never misses the mark, show me the way forward!*

Keep moving, allowing yourself to now go as fast as you can. Run if you can! Repeat Artemis's name over and over. At the peak of your energy say:

WE CAN'T ACTUALLY CONTROL ANYONE

> *Artemis, accept me! Artemis, I join you! May it please you that I connect with you in honour.*

Imagine placing some of that strength and power you now feel into the stone in your hand. Say:

> *I honour you. I will do your work upon this earth to preserve and protect it. I will protect your creatures; I will be strong and independent. Bless me and help me be sincere in this. Mighty huntress, I give you thanks!*

Stop moving and bury the stone in the earth.

Calling in your sovereignty with Pomona

This spell doubles as a blessing for your garden and a nod to developing your own realm and sovereignty. It is becoming justifiably more popular to grow your own food, whether it be a few herb pots in your apartment or a vegie patch in your backyard. You too can take energy of the plenty of Pomona to ensure your harvest is a great one, whether it be big or small!

The spell is best performed under a full moon if possible and can be done on an existing garden or when sowing seeds or seedlings.

You'll need:

* ✳ one red candle
* ✳ a watering can filled with water
* ✳ pruning shears or a small knife
* ✳ a ripe tomato or herbs
* ✳ one green candle.

Light the red candle. Say:

> *Pomona, red-cheeked maiden of plenty*
> *Goddess of the garden, beloved of all*
> *I invite you to tend to my realm*
> *Hear my call!*

Tell Pomona what you would like for your garden and your personal realm. Give her a tour. Tell her about your ripe fruit or wildly growing herbs: how all will be fertilised by the insects, how you'll appreciate the flowers and how you want your home to be beautiful or your business prosperous.

Hold the watering can and think about all this garden of plenty and your life in all aspects being plentiful. Feel the power in this and allow the emotion to rise. Imagine extending this energy into the water. Put the watering can down, hold up the pruning shears or knife and say:

> *I know to grow*
> *I know to glow*
> *I agree to cut and prune*
> *Under the moon.*

Go out to the garden or where your pots are with the tomato or herbs, watering can and shears. Water the garden and say:

> *Grow, grow, in the name of Pomona grow.*

Make a small cut of a dead leaf or dead wood and say:

> *Prune away, cut away, in the name of Pomona, I prune!*

Bury the tomato and say:

> *I offer this to you, Pomona! Thank you.*

Go back and light the green candle. Let both candles safely burn down.

73

V

LOVE IS AN ORGANISING PRINCIPLE

The different kinds of love; love as an organising principle; the tough love of the dark goddesses; influence; forgiveness; liberation; equality; protection; defence

Kali

The god Shiva sees Ma Kali for the first time. He trembles in fear for she is time itself. She is naked because she is infinite and has nothing to hide, as ime is beautiful and terrible all at once. Shiva sees Ma Kali's open mouth and understands that everything degrades and changes before time and time swallows all.

He watches her move across the plain. She wears a small hip skirt featuring human hands that represent all our deeds merging into time. She wears a necklace of skulls that represent all human thoughts – which may be great or poor – and these merge into time. She holds a severed head of a demon in one hand representing all of our personal evils or negative egos and shows that these too are defeated through her and will be suppressed by time.

Shiva sees Ma Kali dancing on flames and ashes blackening her body and knows that everything that is not needed can be purified through her. Anything that is not wanted – the unloved parts, shame, ill deeds, our shadows – all can be handed to her for transformation. He realises that she is compassion itself.

Shiva sees her fully and loves her immediately, completely.

Eros

The universe was but a primordial slush. There was no distinct earth, water, sky, air or sea: just a chaotic cauldron of everything and nothing. Then, infinitely slowly, more evolved. Distinct energies began to form and liberate themselves from the mass. The first organising influence to leave chaos was Eros, love. Before any other element – earth, sky or even water – love came forth first.

Eros became form. Not the chubby, cute cherub of later Christian times was Eros, but a fully fledged virile, beautiful and powerful god of love. In his true form, a stunningly desirable man, he was responsible for the lust and ardour of love as well as the responsibilities such as trust that come hand in hand with it.

Eros travelled the world, bringing love to all things and putting structure and creation into the world.

· WALKING THE PATH ·

Picture Kali. Scared? Exactly. This is what this amazing goddess is all about – a kind of fierceness. The Hindu goddess Kali is fearsome yet has a powerful maternal aspect of protection. She invokes fear in many who do not understand her untamed nature, and for those who do she is welcomed. However, it's this fierceness, this extreme force of nature, that helps us overcome our fears moving forward, to cut through the fears and obstacles we have and to slay our personal demons.

Kali helps us deal with the things that haunt us that are fear based such as jealously, pride and unhealthy anger. She breaks down the illusions of the ego, kills the shadows that do not serve us any longer and therefore frees our true selves. In this way she expresses her tough love for us. Kali can help us negotiate any transition, in particular ones we are afraid and hesitant to make. Remember that while most of her hands contain a weapon there is one that does not. It is showing a peaceful, placating gesture, a signal of her true love for us.

I love the idea that we can go and build structure and reduce chaos with love. The Greeks called upon Eros to attract partners, marriages and even friends. This mighty god will help bring in love, build trust in existing relationships and, if you dare, prise open a heart damaged by loves lost. In his form as Eleutherius, the liberator, he is useful for assistance in freeing ourselves from negative beliefs about sex and trauma.

Imagine if we ran a business through the filter of love. Or ran a country that way. Or instead of choosing greed as a motivator for prosperity we chose love as the organising influence instead.

With love must also come forgiveness, and this is hard to do with love's extreme emotions. In the mythos of Eros and Psyche we can see the results of mistrust and confusion. While love can be a liberating thing it can also be something that cages us. The temptation to misuse the hold we have over others in love relationships can be ever present if we are not truly aligned with our selves in its highest form. We hurt others. We make bad decisions. We may need to forgive as part of our recognition and through self-love and other love. It's worth remembering the following about forgiveness:

* You do not have to forgive; it is a choice.
* True forgiveness occurs in your own time and only you can make it happen.
* Holding a grudge or lots of anger and rage can feel powerful. In some ways it *is* powerful, yet if we want a cleaner space between us and those who have harmed us then seeking a way through those emotions is wise.
* Importantly, forgiveness doesn't mean the person who harmed you gets a free pass. It means you get freedom from the negative associations of the actions of and the actuality of that person who harmed you.
* You can forgive and place the kind of boundary that means this person never gets to again do what they did. You don't go back for more. You do not allow the same circumstances. You stand up for yourself, empower yourself and, in the case of a crime, seek lawful justice if this is apt and available to you.
* Forgiveness starts with ourselves. Remember we speak of power from the inside out. Forgiving ourselves for any part we played in any transgression – and, of course, learning the lesson – is key. Making amends may be a part of this process. We deserve to forgive ourselves because we are human, and we make mistakes if we are actually living our lives in any meaningful way.
* Be kind to yourself.

Finally, I want to share a few things about my experiences with goddesses such as Kali and with Kali herself.

First, during the working do not overthink what you do and say to Kali or other goddesses. She will explode that bullshit so fast you won't know what hit you. Instead, just be honest with what is going on and give it to her warts and all. If you don't quite know what you want to give over tell her that, and she will reach down and take it from you because she knows what has to go even if you don't.

Second, it is highly relieving in my experience to let go and let the goddess. I understand it is difficult to surrender, but in surrendering I do not mean failing or giving up. I mean to hand over control, just as you would let go of control of your body in the water to float on the surface. Let go and you rise.

Third, carried anger appears as many other things than just being angry. Mostly it appears as a kind of resistance, such as procrastination, refusal to focus on self and thus drama/jealousy/gossip/interference in other's lives and distrust and fear of doing positive things. Hand over to Kali everything that feels stuck. Hand over all the burdens that aren't yours, including your need to control others if that is what you are doing.

Do this and she will take it, and I promise life will change for the better.

TASKS

1. Do you feel you express your emotions such as anger, resentment and rage in real time? If not, why not? Be as specific as you can.

2. When we begin to change our lives we can sometimes become overzealous or too careful of making the same mistakes by tipping too far the opposite way. Think about the ways in which you wish to change your life as it is and consider if there are any behaviours that you might be tempted to go too far the opposite way in. Mention this here.

3. Consider this: if you were able to express difficult emotions better in real time, how much better or completely would your life change?

4. Choose one of the answers to question 3 and action it immediately.

5. Is there an advantage to rage?

6. Consider the shadows of the self that you really dislike. What would happen if Kali, in her infinite compassion, destroyed those? What would be the benefit to you?

· MAGICAL WORKINGS ·

Meeting Kali

You'll need:

* ✳ a candle
* ✳ incense
* ✳ a gift for Kali.

Find a quite spot where you won't be interrupted and light the candle and incense. Dedicate your gift to Kali. Get yourself in a comfortable seated or prone position and close your eyes. Take three big breaths. Focus on your base chakra, your sit bone at the base of your spine. Imagine it warm and glowing. Allow the rest of your being to expand and reach out across time and space.

There is no wrong way to do this. Don't think; just allow.

Now you are in a place that is a wide, empty field. It is dark, barely lit, everything is ashes. The moon is in its dark phase. Walking towards you silently is the goddess Kali. She is coming towards you step by step from the horizon. You can take a good look at her as she comes closer. You can hear the clink of her bone skirt as she walks. You can smell the fire and ash. You can see her blue skin, her black tongue. You can see the skulls around her neck. You can experience her fierceness. Her absoluteness. Her timelessness.

She has her hands outstretched in love and compassion to take from you what you most fear. You are her child; she is your cosmic mother. She will protect you, so you give her this – or not. She takes it, burns it to ash. The moon turns to its new aspect.

You thank Kali. She continues on her way. Be aware of how different your body and mind feel then allow your body to return to its grounded form. Be in this time in this body. Open your eyes when you are ready.

You'll need:

*   a black candle
*   pen and paper
*   a small amount of ash placed on a small plate (you can make this by burning some wood, fragrant sandalwood chips or some charcoal and resin
*   a gift for Kali.

Light the candle and say:

> *Great mother Kali, I call upon you to help me reduce and destroy my fears. You, who kills demons. You, who are fearless! Bless me and protect me.*

Chant three times:

> *Om Kali Ma! Jai Kali Ma!*

Out loud, describe the fears you have, what is in the way and what your fears cause you to do. Use specific examples and be honest even though it may be hard to talk about. Know that Kali listens and is responding. Say:

> *Kali, I want my life to be better, yet my fears hold me back. Some of them are big. Some of them are hidden. You, who are change itself, you who defeats the shadow in me, from now show me how to move forward fearlessly. What do I do next to facilitate my change into being more fearless, great Kali?*

Write down any ideas or messages you may receive on the paper. You will action these later. Place your index finger in the ash and anoint your forehead with it in the third eye position between your eyebrows. Say:

> *Kali, thank you for my blessing. I agree to participate and do my part. Thank you!*

Leave your gift on your altar or space.

The ashes ritual

---

* Light a candle and ask for Kali.
* Ahead of time write down what you want Kali to turn to ashes for you, one thing per strip of paper.
* Put all in a flameproof bowl and ask Kali to turn this to ash.
* Set the paper on fire.
* Allow it to burn down, thanking Kali.
* Dip your finger in the ashes and draw a spiral on your forehead.
* Put the rest of the ashes in the garden.
* Promise Kali one action you'll take towards your transformation.

Invocation to Eros

Take a deep breath. Relax. Inhale. Exhale. Draw a bow and arrow on some paper and add a heart shape. Say out loud:

> *You who stepped first from chaos, align me*
> *Eros, I ask for clarity, I ask for your guiding arrow*
> *I pray for a fertile open heartedness*
> *The courage to trust*
> *The wildness of heart to allow a sweet surrender*

> *A letting go of the dusty crust around my soul*
> *A freedom of spirit so I can feel love sweep through me like wind in my hair*
> *Yet*
> *A balance*
> *A healing*
> *A forgiving*
> *A contentment*
> *Eros, hear me.*

Imagine Eros with you now, his mighty wings unfurling and him shooting a painless arrow into your heart. Instantly you feel warmer, more alive and more confident. Thank Eros and place your bow and arrow drawing within your pillowslip on your bed.

VI

FIRST, OBSERVE

*The role of observation in ancient and
indigenous cultures; what we lose when
we are too fast; slow spirituality; utisetta;
cycles; nature deserves observation*

THE MYTHOS

Maui

Maui is the being responsible for introducing fire to man. In fact, he stole it from a bird! Maui and his brothers went fishing in the lagoon and happened to look back at the mountain near the shore, where there was a fire burning. Man had not had fire for many generations as the volcano that supplied the embers had ceased its rumbling. Racing back, Maui found only a wisp of smoke and a family of Alae hens diligently stamping the fire out.

Every day thereafter Maui and his brothers checked for fire but nothing was seen. However, as they paddled out to fish there again, glowing against the mountain, was fire, out of his reach again!

Now Maui had a plan: he decided to wait on shore while his brothers went fishing, but again no fire was seen. Increasingly frustrated, Maui decided to make a life-sized grass doll of himself, and it was this that his brothers paddled out with one fine day. This time as Maui watched he would catch the birds at their fire.

Maui climbed up the mountain and found an Alae just about to begin to make the fire. Not waiting for her to start, in his anger he grabbed her and held her prisoner. Reminding him that if he hurt her the secret would be lost, Maui agreed to desist from detaining her in return for the recipe for fire. The old Alae was smart and again and again tricked Maui into techniques that did not work. Finally, by watching closely, he found fire by rubbing two special sticks together.

As we know, as well as having an adventurous spirit Maui is also quite the mischievous man. 'Come here,' he said to the Alae. 'There is one more thing to rub!' He rubbed the feathers on her head so hard that a bald patch appeared. Ever since that day of discovery Alae mud hens have no feathers upon their heads.

Yemaya

Before the goddess Yemaya was a queen of the sea she was a younger Orisha, or nature spirit. She was very beautiful, and many suitors came a-calling hoping for her hand.

One god, Orunmila, who was very wise and the god of oracles and divination, came to court her. Yemaya looked at him and wasn't impressed: he was old and kind of wrinkled and she paid him no attention. After all, there were better-looking suitors out there, but runmila was determined and decided to seek council from Elegba, who was good at these things. Elegba suggested he bring Yemaya many presents, as at least this would get him some attention.

Orunmila collected many wonderful presents, so many that he was staggering with the sheer weight of them all. He met with Yemaya, and as he got near her the pile of parcels he was carrying tipped over. As it did the force of the collapse turned some of the gifts inside out – and him as well! runmila quickly turned himself back the right way, but Yemaya had seen what he looked like on the inside.

She saw who he really was, and she saw such beauty! Such goodness! Such honesty and love! She chose him and fell in love with him and they married.

FIRST, OBSERVE

· WALKING THE PATH ·

We don't tend to look around much anymore and neither do our kids. We are currently in an epidemic of short-sightedness in children because they don't look at the horizon or far enough into the distance. Instead, their eyes develop while looking closely at screens. This doesn't occur at the same rate, though, for rural children, who engage with the landscape.

When I travelled to the Ecuadorian Amazon a native guide showed us the forest over a few days. The forest is thick but is an unbelievably diverse ecosystem. There are so many different kinds of plants and animals, insects and birds. At times the sound is deafening. As we travelled through the landscape often our guide would put a finger to his lips to quieten us and then point at something he wanted us to see. Most of the time I couldn't see anything. I definitely couldn't see what he was seeing, that's for sure.

I like to think because I do enjoy observing habitats where I live, particularly birds, I would have my eye in on these things, but no. Time and time again he would see something that none of us saw, and it often took a long time for us to find the object of his attention. His powers of observation seemed superhuman. His eyesight was incredible.

After a few days, my eye did come in more clearly. A flash here, a strange movement there, a flick of water, a small glisten, a shine in the sunlight could all lead us to a creature or plant we wanted to see, yet in no way was I able to achieve the depth of observation our guide could no matter how hard I tried. He simply would say that he 'looks for a living'. We should all take that onboard, no?

Like our friend Maui observing the fires of the hens, we can miss a lot because we just do not bother to look. Time and time again Maui's observation and his way of seeing things a different way enabled him to often win through.

Across Polynesia, from New Zealand to Hawaii, we hear stories about the hero Maui. Although the tales differ slightly from island to island, region to region, Maui's exploits have given man fire, invented the kite and even fished up whole islands for man to live upon.

Sometimes depicted as a slightly dishevelled everyman, he manages to outwit his brothers and other opponents in his adventures with his street smarts. Other versions tell of a strong and mighty Maui able to perform superhuman heroic feats, but the link in most of his stories is his curiosity, observation, urge for discovery and help to the community. The bonus is that the stories are usually kind of funny.

However, the stories about Yemaya, the Yorbian goddess, are generally inspiring and beautiful. Again, we see a mythos about really seeing; in this case the true essence of someone rather than forming a firm judgement about their outside appearance.

Yemaya started her life as an Orisha, a river spirit, in Africa. As her people travelled over the ocean in slave ships to other nations she became, over time, a goddess of the sea. Her cult spread to Brazil too and she is still worshipped today in all these lands as a goddess of love. She is said to have watched over her enslaved people on the slave ships and would send dolphins to guide them to shore should the boat be shipwrecked.

Yemaya is often depicted as a mermaid, slipping between the waves with lights woven within her hair. She is also considered to be the nourishing mother aspect of all water. She is said to be an extremely loving goddess and will assist women in particular. Many homes that follow the Santeria faith will have a statuette of Yemaya placed by the woman of the home. She is invoked when the mother's waters break and she is in childbirth. It is said that when Yemaya's waters broke they created the sea, and that every man, woman and sea creature descended from her.

TASKS

1. Observe the lunar cycle each night. Just connect in by looking at the night's phase. Do this for a maximum of five minutes.

2. Go outside and find a leaf, stick, flower or stone. Pick it up and observe it for five minutes. Take a long look at everything about it – yes, even rocks have a smell.

3. Instead of scrolling through your phone when you are outside, take a moment to look around. What aren't you seeing right now?

4. Have you ever been inventive in finding solutions to problems or issues? Have you ever been tricked into doing something, or tricked yourself?

5. Do you ever ignore red flags? Why?

· MAGICAL WORKINGS ·

Invocation for innovation and wonder

Place a fish hook on your altar or go out to a body of water and cast a line with a fish hook attached – no bait, please! Ideally you'll also have some small tropical flowers you can use. Say:

> *Maui, hero and discoverer*
> *Son of Hina*
> *Friend of mankind*
> *Aloha!*

[Throw a flower in the water or on your altar]

> *Maui, I wish to be the hero of my own life and be courageous and*
> *adventurous*
> *Friend of mankind, guide me*
> *Maui, I have a problem that needs a solution*
> *I am frustrated that I cannot find a way through*
> *Friend of mankind*
> *Aloha!*

[Throw a flower]

> *Maui, help me know the secret*
> *Help me discover my strengths*
> *Help me find a way through in joy and good spirits*
> *Friend of mankind*
> *Aloha! Aloha! Aloha!*

[Hold the hook or the line]

> *As I pull this back to me*
> *I know what I need will be hooked and brought to me for my use.*
> *Aloha, Maui!*

Pull the hook back in and know that you are now in possession of all you need. Thank Maui and act on the messages you received.

Yemaya's boats

This is a ritual based on the traditional activity of sending boats filled with wishes to Yemaya. This spell must be done by the sea or river. An optimum time is dusk.

You'll need:

* paper or leaves to make a boat
* a small tealight candle
* a silver gift to Yemaya such as a pearl or a sea shell.

Ahead of time, think about your wish and have it in your mind in a clear and concise fashion and make your boat. Write your wishes on the boat or draw symbols upon it that represent those desires.

Place the candle inside the boat but be careful you don't burn the boat when it's time to light it. Carry it down to the water along with your gift to Yemaya. Say:

> *Yemaya, Yemaya, Yemaya*
> *Silvery goddess of the sea*
> *Moon blessed*
> *She who responds*

> *Goddess of women and wishes*
> *Please hear my voice!*
> *Yemaya, I ask you to grant my wish/es and help me flow like the incoming tide towards my highest good. I humbly offer a gift to you.*

Throw the gift into the water then place your feet in the water and tell Yemaya of your wish. Don't hold back, but keep it crisp and clear.

Light the tealight and set the boat into the water. Be mindful of your safety, but if possible allow the boat to be placed past the first small waves. Say:

> *I know you hear me. My wish comes to you!*

Watch as your boat of wishes travels towards Yemaya. Watch it bobbing up and down over the waves, glowing in the dusk until she takes it below the sea to her. Express your gratitude, as she will now grant your wish! Act upon any ideas you may have that come to mind to hasten this.

Consider these questions:

* When was the last time you had yourself a real adventure? What happened, or are adventures for someone else?
* Do you have an active sense of humour and what do you find funny? Do you seek laughter and joy?
* Do you give up when obstacles or resistance forms? What is your usual strategy and does this work for you?
* Have you ever been inventive in finding solutions to problems or issues? Have you ever been tricked into doing something or tricked yourself?

VII

WELCOME THE MYSTERIOUS

The power of 'I don't know'; what are mysteries?; the mysteries matter in spiritual pathways; we don't know what we don't know; we don't have to show everything all the time; enjoy not knowing; mysteries are spiritual catalysts

Vesta

One of the most magnificent buildings in ancient Rome had in its heart a mighty flame. The temple was round, and the flame reflected dancing upon the warm white walls. The fire had been struck from two sacred pieces of wood, blessed in the name of the goddess who protected Rome and all her people. Flames from this fire were brightening every home in Rome, protecting all.

The priestesses tended the flame, singing and performing the rites and ensuring that the *foculus*, this mighty hearth that represented the spirit of Rome itself, was strong. These women, who were the guardians of this hearth, were also the guardians of the laws and most important documents of Rome and all its families. Wills, title deeds, agreements, business deals and even treaties between nations were held and witnessed by the priestesses, who were seen to be beyond reproach.

Treated like no other women – educated, free, venerated – they gave themselves to the service of the virgin goddess and to Rome. They too, like her, remained virgins, unencumbered by family and dedicating themselves to the good of all citizens.

Vesta is the Roman goddess of home and hearth. A key protective deity in Rome, the hearth would always be lit at her temples and at any shrines that were created in her honour. Ideally, these fires would not be allowed to go out, showing not only tribute to the goddess but symbolising the warmth and comfort of the home to its family.

Hekate

One bright day, as Persephone was enjoying the sunshine outdoors with her maiden friends including Hekate, she came upon a particularly stunning narcissus flower. As she picked it, a great rumbling occurred and Hades arose from the ground and seized Persephone. Persephone struggled but was overpowered and taken down to the underworld.

Only the goddess Hekate and the sun god Helios heard her screams although Hekate, being in her cave, did not see who had taken her. As she was a devoted and loving mother, Demeter began a frantic search all over the earth for her daughter but to no avail. She could think of nothing else besides her daughter, so she began to neglect her role of grain giver and earth mother and the farmers' fields began to die. Her anguish deepened and she forbade the earth to produce, leaving the earth barren and cold.

Soon the people began to die and cry to Zeus to assist them. Hekate suggested that Zeus speak to Helios, who may have seen what happened. Helios told Zeus of Hades's act and Zeus demanded that Hades return Persephone through Hermes. Hekate lit torches for her friend to guide her home.

In the underworld, meanwhile, Persephone missed the world above but began to like Hades a little. He offered her the queenship. When he kindly presented a pomegranate to her to eat and she accepted. She had consumed six seeds from the glossy, ruby-red fruit when Zeus's demand reached them. According to the Fates, if someone consumes food or drink in the underworld they must stay there, so it seemed as though Persephone would have to stay in the world of shadows. Zeus, however, came up with a compromise: Persephone would spend half the year with Hades and six months above with Demeter.

Persephone returned to the earth and her mother, and she was guided by Hekate's torches. Hekate joined them and welcomed Persephone back, and from that time Hekate became Persephone's

propolos or guide and her companion on her annual journey to and from the underworld.

Demeter, in her joy, resumed her work with the fields and life again appeared on earth. However, when Persephone returned to Hades six months later Demeter grieved and again left the world barren.

· WALKING THE PATH ·

There is a profound beauty in the darkness, the unseen, the mysterious. In a world where we think we know everything, where the current paradigm tells us that everything is brightly exposed with nothing unknown, choosing to still commune with possibility and the admission that there is indeed some mystery remaining in the darkness is vital for our balance and harmony as humans.

Our ancient ancestors knew this. Their mythos and stories are certainly not just stories of love and light (lite), but very often of darkness, fear, monsters, creatures of the unknown and journeys into and out of the underworld. These are stories with a truth that have echoed down through the millennia, warning us about poor behaviour, revenge, hubris, disrespect of the gods or the land itself and simultaneously calling us to our better natures through the encouragement of resilience, courage, faith, restoration, loyalty and kindness.

For some time now, especially in some aspects of the wellness and spiritual communities, there is a strange over-compensation where everything has to be all light, totally positive and irrevocably blemish free. There is a pressure to be wide-grinningly happy all the time, and even when we are sick or get injured or have trauma it's thought that all this somehow was invited by us through not being positive enough.

This toxic positivity, this reaching for an impossible perfection and the quiet victim blaming that this suggests: where exactly has this gotten us? I would suggest that it leads us into more pain and confusion, guilt and suffering.

One of the pioneers of analytical psychology, the famous psychoanalyst Carl Jung, once said: 'Everyone carries a shadow and the less it is embodied in the individual's conscious life, the blacker and denser it is.' What he is suggesting is that we are not immediately conscious of the bits of ourselves we may not like or wish to show yet they still show up and are active in our lives. Hiding them doesn't mean they go away; in fact, they can grow ever

101

stronger by being ignored. So what can we do? The best thing is to make them more conscious, to seek them out and maybe even make friends with them.

If we decide to seek or engage with these unconscious aspects of ourselves these darker shadows, these ill-formed, half-created, seemingly ugly monsters of our unconscious, perhaps we can refine them or reshape them into something exquisitely useful and beautiful. Perhaps we could grow to love them because they are the wholeness of who we actually are.

What if the shadowy fear of rejection we harbour deep in the darkness can be transformed once we see it into the formation of a confident, discerning and independent self? What if the ball of self-hatred that lies within the stagnant dark waters can be undone, unravelled and made new into a deep and unashamed appreciation of self?

We live, though, in a time of rampant social media in which we pick partners by scrolling left or right, when we may spend hours skimming literally hundreds of little vignettes of life from people we will most likely never meet or have deeper connections with – yet many of these vignettes are deeply personal or at least are crafted to look that way. This is a time when we get influenced by showing and telling everything we can, a time when the word 'oversharing' got invented. But what if we became a little more mysterious? What if we embraced not knowing a little more, that we don't show everything all of the time? That we allowed the sacred uncertainty of life – surprise – to play through again? How about we decide that it's okay to say we don't know? That it is perfectly fine to not share with all and sundry certain sacred moments and loves?

This was and still is in some circles how the mysteries within a cult tradition were formed. Only initiates were shown the rituals, ceremonies and rites because they were deeply prepared for them. It wasn't just that you could look up a ritual to keep Rome safe through Vesta on the internet; you had a group of priestesses who only knew how. We don't actually know what the rites were for the Vestal priestesses in the service of their fire goddess Vesta, we don't know precisely what the mysteries of the rituals and resulting statecraft were, but we do know quite a bit about how important that kind of secrecy was. It was important enough that a priestess of Vesta could lose her life for revealing it.

Vesta was a key protective goddess in the Roman pantheon, and every Roman home would have contained a shrine to her no matter how humble at their hearth. The hearth was the place where food was prepared and bread baked, and where warmth and a source of light came from. It was the spiritual heart of the home and family. The woman of the home was the one responsible for the rites to Vesta, keeping her family safe and well blessed.

We know to have a Vestal in the family was prestigious and a mark of good character. We know that the Vestals themselves were paid clergy. These women could serve the goddess only if they took a vow of chastity for 30 years, thus the modern term for them, the 'Vestal virgins'. Should the Vestal break their vows, including telling the secrets of the rites or the documents in their care, they were killed by being buried alive. There were advantages though: the Vestals were given freedoms that women of that time were not commonly endowed with and were to educated and free to travel within Rome unaccompanied.

It is no wonder that after their 30 years of service few decided they wanted a normal Roman woman's life of marriage, and being under the thumb of the *pater familias* wasn't for them. Most stayed in the service of the goddess until their deaths with their high status and word beyond reproach, keeping the flame alight.

This torch of illumination is a strong theme in mythos. We can heal through shining a torch within the darkness to illuminate it. We can find our real and most empowered selves through journeying down into the unknown, choosing to go swimming in the dark, deep waters and walking the path in what may feel like the death-stalked atmosphere of the underworld. Remember even the Bible speaks about walking through the shadow of death: not actual death but the shadow of death, something that feels like death yet we overcome it.

The Greek goddess Hekate is possibly one of the most mysterious and oldest of all the Greek goddesses and one of the most loved and feared as

103

a torch bearer. Said to be the daughter of the Titans' Perses and Asteria (starry), Hekate is a goddess of the sea, of the night and of witchcraft and, as a torch bearer, of illumination. Her name translates into 'she who works her will'.

For a long time the so-called dark goddesses got a bad rap. People thought that if a goddess was of the dark or looked a certain way – that is, scary – then they were evil or nasty. The Christianisation of certain mythos twisted many stories as well, in particular those of deities, usually female, who were perhaps magic makers, sorceresses, too independent or feisty, who were remade into evil and dangerous spirits. Stories of Circe, Kali, The Morrigan, Morgan le Fay and Medusa are examples, and when we look at a complex figure such as Hekate it is important to understand that paradoxically a dark deity can actually be an illuminator.

When Persephone was taken by Hades into the underworld and Zeus and Demeter negotiated for her return, it was her friend, the goddess Hekate, who lit torches for her to guide her home. Similarly, in 340 BCE the greatest general of the age, Philip II of Macedon, was ready to complete the attack on the Byzantines and their allies the Athenians after a lengthy siege of the walls of Byzantium.

It was a dark and wet moonless night and Philip thought this would be the perfect undercover foil for a final push and surprise attack on the city. He believed the dark moon hid everything, so his troops prepared for an assault on the city and were very confident of success. Happily for the Byzantines the patroness of the city, Hekate, also favoured nights such as this and was watching.

As Philip's soldiers began forming their attack, Hekate lit her bright torches in the inky heavens. This unexpected bright light awoke all the watchdogs of the town and they began to loudly bay and bark. The garrison was awoken and they foiled Philip's attack. This was the turning point in the siege. To thank Hekate the city erected a special statue to her referred to as the *lampadephoros* (torchbearer). It was erected on a hill above the Bosphorus Sea to commemorate Hekate's defensive aid.

Hekate literally carries a torch even though she stands in the opaqueness at a crossroads or under a moonless night sky. Yes, she carries a torch when she is striding through the darkness of the deep underworld, yet she is actually lighting the way out for all of us. This magnetic goddess invites you to travel the shadows with her under her wise guidance, as she brings you to the light. When you are ready to leave the underworld after your shadow work, it is she who will protect you as you return to the world better than ever.

TASKS

1. Think about your own shadow, the hidden things you keep quiet. Pick one of these unwanted behaviours or patterns and identify one aspect you would like to transform.

2. What is an aspect of yourself you used to not like but you do now?

3. Do you do ritual? Ceremony? Spells? What do you think is helpful about these?

4. Try and reduce your time on social media, particularly random doom scrolling, by 10 per cent this month. Use your time elsewhere.

5. Observe how much gossip and gossip masquerading as news or entertainment there is around you. Understand that this gotcha journalism and exposure to an industry that can be damaging. Is there something else you could be consuming?

· MAGICAL WORKINGS ·

Blessing for the home with Vesta

Traditionally, each Roman home had a small space dedicated to Vesta, called a vestibule, or a hearth. While you possibly don't have these things in your home, if you like the energy of Vesta you may consider setting up a small shrine somewhere in your home or even within your fireplace if you have one.

You'll need:

* a piece of paper and a pen
* some fresh flowers and a vase
* some ash or sand
* a large candle in any colour but gold; flame colours are favourites
* a small flameproof bowl
* incense.

Ahead of time, think about what you would like to wish for positively for your family and home. You might want protection, joy, happiness, prosperity and good health, for example. Write this down on a piece of paper.

Arrange the flowers in a pretty vase and place it on the area you are doing this blessing. Trace a circle with the ash or sand and place the candle in the centre. Light the candle and say:

> *I call upon Vesta*
> *Vesta of Rome!*
> *I call your blessed name*
> *She of the sacred flame*
> *She of the centre of the earth*

> *She who protects all around the holy hearth.*

Pick up the paper and read what you want Vesta to grant you. Do this out loud. Imagine having all of these things for your home and family. Take your time. This feels good!

Read the paper again and say:

> *I release these requests to you, Vesta, and know that they will be granted.*

Burn the paper over the candle flame then pop it into the bowl so you don't burn yourself.

Thank Vesta for her help and burn the incense. Allow the candle to safely burn for at least a few hours in her honour.

Invocation to Hekate

Be respectful!

This ritual can be done at any crossroads where three pathways or roads meet. You'll probably find a simple crossroads at the edge or your property where your path and gate meet the public path or at the end of your own street. As I approach the crossroads I often like to call Hekate's name three times out loud. You will often hear a dog bark or the wind rise or whistle as you do this, which shows she is present.

You'll need:

* ✳ three red candles
* ✳ some dog fur: just pat a dog and collect the shed hairs
* ✳ some ground good-quality incense such as frankincense.

Light the first candle and say:

Great goddess Hecate, bright headed, twin flamed
You who rule over the crossroads, our past, present and future
The dark, the crescent and the full
Help me now
Illuminate my path
Show me the way!

Place the dog hairs at the crossroads and light the second candle. Say:

Great goddess Hekate Apotropaic
Of dark and night, many named!
You who visit the underworld
Show me the way through
Come what may!

Ask Hekate to assist you with clarity and the illumination of issues in your life. Know the goddess is listening. Light the third candle and say:

I pay you tribute, almighty wise goddess
I ask that this small flame join yours,
Spreading light to the darkest corners of my shadow
Bring me peace and wisdom and a resolution to my problems
If it be for the good of all and your will.

Light the incense and let it burn down, relaxing in the energy at the crossroads. Express your gratitude, blow out the candle and leave only the dog hairs there.

The illumination ritual

Sometimes we don't know what we don't know. This ritual with Hekate will help.

You'll need:

* a candle
* a gift for Hekate including a shell and some garlic
* a piece of paper and a pen
* red string
* honey.

Light the candle and place the gift for Hekate on your altar. Write down where you need support or guidance to go forward. Roll the paper up in a ball and tie it with the string, then bury it in the ground. Add the honey to the top.

Ask Hekate for one action you can take. This may come in a dream or as an urge to take some kind of action.

The traditional Deipnon

The Deipnon ritual has been performed in Greece for Hekate since ancient times. It consists of three main parts:

* a meal that was set out at a crossroads, usually in a shrine outside the entryway to the home
* an expiation sacrifice, a kind of personal penance or amends
* purification of the household.

VIII

THE CONTINUOUS GETTING OF WISDOM

(OR HAVING AN OPEN MIND BUT NOT OPEN ENOUGH THAT YOUR BRAIN FALLS OUT)

Knowledge and wisdom; continual learning; black and white thinking; mythos and logos; faith; critical thinking; focus; play; magic

THE MYTHOS

Odin

Mimir, the Rememberer, was the shadowy being who guarded the well of Wyrd at the base of the tree of life, Yggdrasil. The magic waters gave the imbiber unmatched wisdom. Odin, the all-father, approached Mimir for a drink. Mimir told Odin he could have a drink but that he would have to give up one of his eyes for the privilege. Odin gave up one of his eyes for the wisdom contained in the well.

Athena

Metis, the goddess of canny thought, insight and sharp wisdom, was also beautiful and she caught the eye of Zeus. He lay with Metis, but he immediately feared the consequences because the great Titans Gaia and Ouranos had prophesised that Metis would bear children wiser than he himself. This, of course, would not do! Therefore he tricked pregnant Metis into becoming a fly so he could consume her. This he did, and she was a fly inside him and it seemed Metis had been tricked badly – but is that so?

Metis caused terrible headaches for Zeus and of course he could hear her voice, just like his own, inside his head giving advice. The pain in his head was so terrible that he went to the god of innovation and the forge, the strong Hephaestus, and begged him to cleave his head open with a labrys, a double-headed Minoan axe. Screaming in pain, Zeus only found relief when the axe struck.

Athena leaped fully grown with a shout from Zeus's head, dressed in her silver armour, and pealed to the broad sky her clarion cry of war. It was said that the old gods all trembled to hear it. Upon first sight, though, Zeus loved his daughter. He saw the magnificence in her and sensed she was different. He loved her wise counsel and intelligence. He looked into her light grey eyes and saw an ideal, and realised that here was a daughter who could only be an asset.

And Metis? She decided to stay within Zeus and whisper wisdom to him.

· WALKING THE PATH ·

I have always loved the story of the Norse god Odin giving up his eye for wisdom as well as being quite horrified by it. Here was the most powerful god in the Norse pantheon striking out his own eye for a chance to be wiser. We know there was a good reason other than just the getting of general wisdom for him to do so, as he knew Ragnarök, the end of the world cycle, was coming. If Odin could learn more about how it would happen and when then the all-father, in his protective role, perhaps could work out a way to halt it or at least ensure some of the powers of good survived. Mimir, too, understood the value of wisdom and wasn't going to give it away just because the great Odin had simply asked for it.

Wisdom is worth getting. Every year on my birthday I decide I am going to learn something new for the year. I figure eventually I'll be an old lady, so I may as well be an interesting and hopefully wise old lady.

Some years the thing I learn I have not taken further, and it hasn't been something I resonate with at all. I've experienced it, but in doing so I saw it wasn't for me. I don't regret it because I have been exposed to something different and I have learned something new. However, some of the birthday learnings have enriched my life so very much I can hardly imagine not ever doing them again. They have become integral parts of my life, giving me huge amounts of pleasure and some even helping me express my purpose in the world. I would never be feeling this richness unless I took a risk answering my curiosity and had a go.

I think part of the reason I don't particularly worry about learning is that I have made it a habit: I have beginner's mind, and as a beginner at something means I have experienced it as being playful, something that isn't full of pressure. I know that many people feel opposite to that, that learning something from scratch is hard and full of stress and pressure, but I do believe this is a state and an expectation we often place upon ourselves wrongly.

Like Zeus, we can be nervous about smarter people. We might be afraid to play with people who challenge us in this way but look what happened

114

when Athena, the goddess of wisdom, was actually born. Zeus immediately felt love for her. Wisdom was his ally, a strength, not something or someone to compete with!

A good teacher will make learning enjoyable, especially at the start, and no one expects a beginner to be perfect yet sometimes all our insecurities about learning may swirl into play and we are discouraged or, worse, we don't try. We may get scared, but I would invite you when you think about the getting of wisdom to allow the wonder to seep through the fear, to allow that anticipation of what could be to dominate the inertia.

Notice I choose to learn a single skill or have a certain experience, not press myself to do 100 things – although that indeed may happen in joy! We can, bit by bit, gather experiences and lessons and eventually we have a lot of them as life progresses. We can read books regularly, we can listen to podcasts, we can go to free lectures, we can decide we will deep dive into a subject for a short time. We can prioritise this. We can decide that the getting of wisdom matters. Most importantly to me is that we examine all sides of something we are interested in if we can with as many good-quality sources as possible. We must avoid black and white thinking at all costs because this is not wisdom, but opinion.

Right now we have more information available to us through the internet than at any time in human history. Do we have a wiser population? I don't actually think so. Why? Because the very basis of learning about many subjects is learning critical-thinking skills so we can separate the wheat from the chaff. Many people cannot tell the difference between a piece of propaganda and something factual. They get turned on by someone brash who seems brave for seeming to tell it how it is when all that is being expressed is an extreme black and white view. Plus, it all gets validated through the algorithms that feed them more of the same bias on social media. It's a toxic bubble of sameness. We have forgotten the magnificent art of finding the grey.

In the wellsprings of places that valued learning and innovation in the ancient world they didn't just value one kind of learning. In Athens, for example, certainly an innovative place, they strove to educate their

young with both logos (logic) and mythos (stories, poems and art with a truth). Today those two aspects of learning seem to be at an opposing rather than a weaving point. Logos is seen as the enemy of mythos, which has again come to be seen as an untruth or fantasy rather than a way of seeing more deeply.

We must learn to go deeper for wisdom. We must learn to go slower to get a fuller picture. We must observe, and experientially understand. History is littered with major mistakes in battle or in policy because the decision-makers didn't have or even want the full picture. The cycles of nature run slowly, day by day, and they are great teachers for us when it comes to progressive wisdom.

This brings me to the idea of being able to change our minds with more information without shame. I think we all know people who hold really stagnant views, who will not change their view even with new, truthful and indisputable information. I might say indisputable, but dispute they will anyway. They might say things such as 'There is no truth' or 'No one knows, so my opinion is as valid as yours.' Well, yes, there are great mysteries in the world – yay! – but there are also truths.

If I place a pot of water on the stove till it boils and then instruct you to place your hand in that boiling water for a minute I would say there is a pretty universal truth there of what will happen to your hand. You will burn it, and it will be a severe burn. We can talk about different dimensions and time continuums and how severe or not the burn can be, but the bottom line is that putting your hand where your beliefs are means you are not be a wise person to place it in the boiling pot.

In the spiritual world, maybe more than other areas, we have a lot of misinformation. It's a jungle out there right now. Using this example, we may have someone who says the body doesn't matter and their spirit doesn't burn, so it's okay. Someone might say their spirit guide or a demon told them to put their hand in the pot. Some will tell you they have ascended and they have a code for that, so there is no need to put their hand in the pot. Someone might tell you that their god requires them to place their hand in the boiling water as a test of faith. Some will tell you that science is the enemy and that water is natural and it could never hurt you. I could go on, but the only wise reason for not putting your hand in the pot is the reason that it will hurt you badly, and you learned this from your parents probably when you were small. This is indeed a truth.

One of the frustrating things about being out of the broom closet for me is the presumption that folks like me are loopy, ungrounded and, let's say, perhaps a little stupid. Perhaps this is the same for you. There is a presumption that because I do what I do I must believe all kinds of crazy things. I would love a dollar for every person that has said, after learning that my husband is a specialist medical doctor, 'Oh, wow, opposites attract, huh? How does that work?'

This is insulting, and they don't even realise the negative inference until I ask them to explain what they mean. Invariably they begin to say something along the lines of 'Oh, he is well educated and you ...' or 'He is so scientific and you are ...' or 'He would have to be so grounded to do what he does ...', then they splutter and stop as they realise what they are saying and begin to backtrack with 'But you know what I mean ...'

Well, actually, I don't.

Forgetting that I, too, have a formal higher education and that the word 'author' is on my tax as my official occupation, as a pagan I probably have a more grounded view of the world than most. What I don't know the answer to I'll proudly state, and I like making mistakes so I learn faster and better. I was asked recently on a radio program what I think happens after death. I was on a mixed panel of medicos and religious folks but I was the only one who stated 'I don't know. No one knows for sure.' Then I added 'But right now I think we get our energy recycled. You know, like the first law of thermodynamics: energy can be transformed from one form to another but can be neither created nor destroyed.'

There was a blip of silence – crickets – and the host made a crack that the most scientific statement of the day had been made by the witch on the panel. One of the doctors expressed a very Christianised view that he would see his god if all went well for him. Did I always feel this way about

THE CONTINUOUS GETTING OF WISDOM

death? No. Was I wrong before? No, but I think differently now, and I keep my mind open about a change in that view in the future.

I think it is a wise person who can say 'I thought this way once but now, with more information, I now think this way.' This, by the way, is part of the scientific method: it is ongoing, progressive and actually open minded, and we can do this same kind of progression bit by bit organically or formally all our lives should we wish. Learning doesn't have an end date.

There is a great story about the Roman emperor and Stoic Marcus Aurelius, considered to be one of the wisest men of his generation, in his old age walking off all the time to listen and learn from the different philosophers and teachers in the forum. When questioned about this he laughed and said that he goes 'to learn that which I do not yet know'.

All of us have plenty we do not yet know, and having a hunger to discover these things actually puts us on a path to wisdom.

TASKS

1. Are you afraid of making mistakes?
2. List here what you yearn to learn.
3. Do you have any negative beliefs around learning?
4. What are your stagnant views? Is there wriggle room for revision?
5. Choose something new to learn. Book it now. Start.

⋆ MAGICAL WORKINGS ⋆

Invocation for Athena's wise counsel

Collect a symbol of Athena, anything with an owl on it – even a picture, a statuette of her, a feather representing an owl, olives or a picture of a war helmet.

You'll need:

* ✳ a white or blue candle
* ✳ a piece of paper and a pen
* ✳ a small ceramic bowl
* ✳ a sprig of fresh rosemary
* ✳ a teaspoon of olive oil.

Light the candle and say out loud:

> *Bright-eyed Athena, free daughter of Zeus*
> *Ever wise, I ask that you hear my call*
> *I place gifts for you here* [place the symbol(s) of Athena down in front of the candle]
> *I ask you to bless me with your wisdom and strategic insight.*

Write on the piece of paper what area you would like more wisdom in and say:

I make my way, I take action but I need your divine assistance with this [state what is written on the paper]. I release this to you knowing that you will give me the guidance I need and that you will show me clearly and promptly what to do. I only need listen.

Burn the piece of paper in the bowl and chant three times:

Wise, wise Athena
Bright eyed and clear
Increase my clarity
Reduce my fear.

Crush the sprig of rosemary to release the aroma and say:

Let me remember your wisdom and your support, and know I have it within myself. In your example I move forward.

Dip your finger in the olive oil and anoint your forehead with it. The goddess will bless you and assist you.

Blow out the candle with thanks.

IX

LOOK TO YOUR OWN VIRTUE AND OFFER PROTECTION AND JUSTICE

TO THOSE WHO NEED YOUR SUPPORT

Your focus should be on developing your own virtue; traditional role of a priestess in protection and healing; the role of justice; compassion and forgiveness

THE MYTHOS

Ma'at

Within the ancient Egyptian view of the world the goddess Ma'at is a bringer of the law unto chaos. Every natural law in the universe was created and judged by Ma'at, thus she is the law even among other deity.

Maat's power decided upon the movements of the tides, seasons and rotations and pathways of the planets and stars. She saw all. It was she who made the final judgement of a soul upon death, so naturally she was respected by all who were living on the earth plane. Ma'at was recognised by the universe as a principal and element and a process in that she was enacted in the lives of the Egyptians.

It was said that once death occurred the body journeyed under the care of Anubis or other underworld protectors and presented to Ma'at in Duat, the underworld. The soul was housed within the heart, and it was this heart that was weighed by Ma'at on a set of golden scales. Her white ostrich feather was the counterbalance to the soul. If the soul was light-hearted and thus had respected all the creator's laws, that soul was admitted to the afterlife to enjoy eternal life and eventual reincarnation. If, however, the soul was found to be heavy-hearted and weighed more than Ma'at's feather that soul was banished forever and eaten by the terrifying goddess Ammit.

Thor awakened one morning to find his hammer, Mjölnir, missing. Little did he know that King Prymr of the Jötnar had stolen it as the bait in a trap to blackmail the gods into granting him the hand of the beautiful goddess Freya in marriage.

Thor thought this theft was not fair and sought to get his hammer back. He found his brother Loki and they discussed what to do. Thor at first wanted to go to war against Prymr and take back the hammer by force. After all, everyone knew the hammer was his to wield. Loki, though, convinced Thor there might be another way to get the hammer back, more through strategy than force. Thor agreed and let his anger fall away, for he knew that justice would be done. They went to find Freya to borrow her winged cloak to help speed things up.

Loki flew around in the cloak until he came upon Prymr, who engaged him in conversation. Loki acted innocent and soon ascertained that the hammer was buried underground. He asked Prymr whether he would just do the right thing and return the hammer but got a hard 'No' from the Prymr. Loki relayed Prymr's ultimatum concerning marriage to Freya to Thor.

After visiting Freya again and asking whether she would marry Prymr and getting quite the mouthful from her in response – of course! – the brother gods of Aesir gathered to discuss their strategy further. It was suggested that Thor should dress in disguise as Freya, covered in a bridal veil. Disguised like this he might well get close enough to his hammer to regain it without much bloodshed. Thor was suitably outraged, but the clever Loki convinced him of the wisdom of this play and so the bride was presented.

Prymr happily greeted them all and invited them to a great feast. Thor, ever the big warrior, began to shovel food through his veil at a great rate, prompting Prymr to question 'Freya's' hunger. Loki confidently answered that Freya had starved herself in eagerness of the coming

125

nuptials. Unable to control his lust, Prymr peeked behind the veil only to be met by a set of fiery savage eyes not fit for a maiden. The king again questioned Loki about why his bride wasis this way. Loki smiled and told Prymr it wass because she hadn't slept for eight nights in her excitement about meeting him.

Finally, it was time for the ceremony and the Jötnar brought out Mjölnir to lay it on 'Freya's' lap to sanctify her prior to the marriage vows. Of course, Thor now had his chance and grabbed his hammer and threw off his wedding gown. Prymr was soundly defeated and was the laughingstock of all who had gathered there. Mjölnir was rightly returned to Thor.

· WALKING THE PATH ·

The Norse had a great love for the god Thor. He was considered to be a humble god, a kind of deity for the everyman. The beloved first son of Odin, he was fair and was a god people could turn to for justice. Thor was a god of contrasts, a kind of bro god but one who cared about people and had great compassion for those who suffered injustice.

A protector of humans, beloved for his powers over fertility, he was also known for his hot temper, and not only was he a god of action but he was also a poet in a culture that greatly appreciated orators, storytellers, musicians and poets. Yet, as the god of storms, Thor captained a chariot pulled by the unlikeliness of two savage, giant goats that thundered raucously across the sky.

When Christianity began its spread across the northlands, Thor's hammer Mjölnir, famous for its lethal power, was adopted as a symbol of defiance by those loyal to the old ways. A description of Mjölnir from the Edda gives us an idea of its power: 'a hammer, which both the frost and the mountain giants know to their cost, when they see it hurled against them in the air, for it has split many a skull of their fathers and kindred. When thrown, it returns to his hand of its own accord.'

In mythos and in many pagan pathways there is an abundance of teachings around having a duty to protect those who are at a disadvantage and those who have suffered injustice. The idea of living a life in which we aim for the highest virtues within ourselves and build up our character from the inside out wis the stamp of the most respected and admired. What are some of those virtues common to these many pathways? Knowing thyself, loving each other, moderation, compassion, righting injustice, finding balance and harmony in nature, displaying courage, continual learning and honouring the gods.

We see through the importance and status of Ma'at, both a goddess and an actual framework of universal laws, just how important living a virtuous life was. To the ancient Egyptians it could mean missing out on eternal life

LOOK TO YOUR OWN VIRTUE AND OFFER PROTECTION AND JUSTICE

should a person have a heavy heart at death, a horrifying result. To align yourself with Ma'at meant also to offer assistance to those who needed it, offer hospitality to strangers and following the good example of the gods, among other laws.

So not all of us can be lawyers, right? Not all of us can be those who set laws in our society, yet we can all radiate fairness and virtue from the inside out. We can, in fact, offer our protection when we can to someone who needs it. We can speak out and speak truth to power if this needs to be done. All of us can find something to improve in this world that will make it a better place for someone. We may not be able to trick a Jötnar into giving Mjölnir back to its rightful owner but we can indeed stand up for someone who is being bullied. We can be a whistle-blower or honest witness. We can create a safe workplace. We can maybe support a kid with a talent who isn't our kid. We can insist on and agitate for more of our tax dollars being used to help more people rather than pull up that ladder behind us.

When I was watching the last Olympic games I had something confirmed to me that I had suspected for a while: that a large proportion of Olympians had relatives who had also been Olympians. We can certainly talk about genetic disposition, but there is a big component of nurture. I, for example, have the body type of a typical middle-distance runner, rower, swimmer, basketballer or cross-country skier. I do not have the body type to be a gymnast, diver, discus thrower or weightlifter, yet I wouldn't really know how good I could do at any of those things because as a kid I wasn't really exposed to them nor was competing or training in those things something on my family radar.

I came from a very modest blue-collar background. One side of my family was on or, in the recent past, below, the poverty line and no one had much education let alone exposure to track and field or sports. My parents couldn't afford weekend athletics or much extracurricular stuff at all. I learned to swim at the Bondi Icebergs because my dad was a member and got free swimming lessons for us and we were able to join the Nippers for free.

Therefore, it makes sense that if you have a family that is, say, into skiing and you get exposed to it at any early age, chances are you will at least be competent at it. If you get the same situation in which you have a family who is used to and has been training for excellence at a high level and, in fact, at world level standards – they know how to do this, what it takes and are connected with the sport and the best people – then you have an advantage. You are in a privileged position.

Let's take education. If your family sees education as a priority or your family was well educated in the past then chances are it will be that the messages you are listening to as you grow are different from those who have no experience with this. Your uncle is a lawyer, your dad is an academic, your mum is a doctor, your aunty is an exceptional woodworker and she apprenticed under the very best. All that shows you is that you could indeed be any of these or more. If you have no one to mentor with or to look up to as an example then how is any of this possible or even, again, on your radar?

There are, of course, exceptions to this: the parents who were disadvantaged in this way, who want more for their kids and impress on them the importance of a good education and will do anything to make sure they have the advantages they didn't. Sometimes, though, it is the fierce will of the child or the innate talent of that child that changes their birth fate. Someone sees them who does recognise their ability and encourages them or gives them the background they need or, even more remarkably, the child themself fumbles around for a bit and finally finds the support they need and does it all themself. It is hard, though, and so many do not make it.

If there was one thing I would love for the society in which I live is that education be once again free. That if you did an apprenticeship at tech or college it was free. That if you did a degree it was free. That if you went to art or film school you paid nothing. That you could get exposed to sports for free. It was once like this in my country and still is in others even today. Those societies where education of this kind is free are some of the most admired and advanced.

Education shouldn't be a privilege, and I think this is a kind of injustice and inequity and it is one of my projects right now to try to work with others to make this happen. I don't know if it will, but at least it's on the agenda with some political parties.

TASKS

1. Have you ever witnessed injustice and did nothing? If you had your time over, would you do it differently?
2. Do you have a cause that you are passionate about that you could offer some of your service to?
3. How can you be more aware of finding balance and equality?
4. In leadership, how do you model virtue and integrity?

· MAGICAL WORKINGS ·

Spell for justice

You'll need:

* a piece of paper and a pen
* a white candle
* a white feather
* a set of scales or two rocks the same size
* a flameproof bowl.

Record your legal or justice issue on the paper. Light the candle and say:

Ma'at, goddess of all order
Queen of justice, fair weigher of souls
I ask for your assistance in resolving a legal issue.

Hold the feather over your heart and say:

You who will grant justice
If it be for the highest good of all
Grant me success and resolution around this issue [tell Ma'at about the issue and where and how you want justice].

Place the feather on one side of the scales or on one of the rocks and say:

I believe my heart is light
I ask that I recognise my part in this [tell Ma'at about your part in this no matter how small].

Hold the piece of paper over the candle to burn it, set it in the flameproof bowl and say:

> I leave this judgement in your hands, great Maat
> Knowing that your justice is swift.

Relax in the knowledge that natural order will be returned. Take the feather outside and release it to the wind, where it will be received by Ma'at. Blow out the candle.

Invocation to Thor

You might want to perform this invocation on a Thursday, Thor's Day, as it will be particularly effective.

Offer mead as a gift to Thor. Turn on some fast-paced music with strong base and make sure it is loud! Feel the music, letting it pour into you pounding each and every cell. When you feel motivated and excited call out:

> I hear your power
> Great Thor of Aesir!
> I see your path
> Iron-handed one!
> I am afraid to take action
> I feel stuck in my boots
> I know no way through
> Bust my rut
> Lend me your belt of strength
> Pump my blood so I can power forward!

Imagine taking action in the direction you wish to and do it! Thank Thor and say:

> *The son of the wise*
> *Swings his hammer*
> *Smashing ignorance and inertia*
> *Making all new in its force*
> *Strong is his honour*
> *Strong are his hands*
> *Courageous is his heart*
> *Shielding all in Midgard.*

Thunder honouring

When you hear thunder, this is Thor's hammer and his goats at work. You may wish to acknowledge him by saying:

> *I hear you, mighty Thor! I honour you!*
> *Pave my way! Protect my way!*
> *Almighty Thor, your gifted power makes me open my mouth in delight*
> *And smile a wolfen grin*
> *My face tingles*
> *My skin feels like it can't contain me*
> *I want to swing a sword, run till I drop*
> *Head towards mountains, laugh out loud*
> *Asgard lives here!*

X

ANYTHING GREAT REQUIRES A SACRIFICE

*The lie of doing it all; choosing; discernment;
saying 'No' as a full sentence; release;
reciprocity; protecting your choices*

THE MYTHOS

Odin

The great god Odin watched as the Wyrd magic of the tree of life and the Norns unfolded as they always did as they carved the runes of prophesy into Yggdrasil. He wanted to increase his knowledge and his wisdom and envied the Norns their power of knowing, but knew the sacred runes only revealed themselves to those who were worthy enough and willing to make sacrifices for their knowledge.

To prove himself Odin hung himself from a branch of the tree, pierced himself in the side with a spear and looked at nothing but the base of the tree where the runes would appear. For nine days and nine nights, without so much as a sip of water, Odin suffered. He forbade any of the other gods to help him. Finally, hovering between death and life and between his lower and higher self, the runes began to reveal themselves and their meanings to him:

> *Then I was fertilised and became wise.*
> *I truly grew and thrived.*
> *From a word to a word, I was led to a word*
> *From a work to a work, I was led to a work.*

Ix Chel

The woman was oiled and flowers put into her hair. She was close to her birthing time. The sweat bath, solid and womb shaped, was prepared and the rainwater barrels gathered ready for the purging steam. Prayers to the jaguar goddess Ix Chel were offered. The woman would enter the sweat bath for some days until her labour began. She heard songs of her ancestors. Songs of the tribe. Songs of the gods and especially of Ix Chel, she who granted the birth and she who would aid the birth. Powerful stories of life were told to fill her baby's spirit.

She would begin her labour and sweat for the release. She would then leave the sweat bath and give birth outside with songs being sung of letting go. Offerings would be made to the jaguar goddess to celebrate the birth, then the mother would re-enter the steam bath to purge her of the afterbirth and any toxins in her body. She would leave the sweat bath a mother, no longer a maiden, one day to be a grandmother.

· WALKING THE PATH ·

At the beginning of this book I spoke about service and I spoke about the differences between service and servitude. I spoke about the priestesses' core act of being of service and to this, unfashionable as it may sound, a sacrifice is necessary to all great things. It is a fallacy to say you can have it all, all the time, but you do not need to be a martyr about it. Let me give you an example.

Being an author and creatrix, I run workshops to help all kinds of folks birth their big works. I do this through the filter of paganism and the priestess. It's fun, and folks seem to do well after and go on to produce very cool stuff. Often I have writers in the room and sometimes they tell me they have so many great ideas or they have three or four unfinished manuscripts in their drawer. They say this like it is a good thing. When I ask them why they haven't completed the work or grounded those ideas in a piece of work they give me all kinds of reasons, all of which are valid to them. Many of these reasons are about what I call 'priority'.

When I mention that I don't think they are making their writing a priority they often say something such as: 'No, Stacey, you don't understand. I really want to write a book.' I ask them: 'Do you want to have a book or do you want to write a book, because they are very different from each other?'

Writing a book, particularly your first book, when it's more likely that authoring is not your full-time job takes sacrifice. It takes time, headspace, bum glue and a really strong work ethic. It can be distinctly unpleasant and sometimes utterly demoralising. It takes courage to choose to stay at home and write rather than go out with your buddies to dinner after work or choose to stay awake at night for an extra hour after the kids go to bed and get some writing time in. It's often not fun. It's a sacrifice for something bigger and it's a clear investment in yourself and what you can do. It's showing faith in your vision.

When I wrote my first book I was working a very intense corporate job that I would also have to travel for. I worked very odd hours. I had

138

a serious relationship. Every moment of my time outside work was precious, yet I placed a structure around my life to get the book done. I wanted to write a book. It still took me longer, way longer than I thought because I had never done it before. I missed out on fun, sleep, down time. My relationship suffered because he didn't understand what I was doing and why, especially when I had a solid and lucrative career already. He didn't like that he wasn't my main focus at that time.

Like Odin, I had my time of suffering but I got what I wanted. I wrote a book; it didn't just appear. There was labour, and that labour meant something else had to go. If I hadn't written the first book it would have meant you would not be reading this book now. The book began a cascade of changes in me that allowed me to be bigger, do more of the work of service and release what ultimately didn't matter so much. My life is now unrecognisable from what it was pre-book.

To protect my focus I had to learn to say 'No' better. I had to learn how to say 'No' as a complete sentence. Yes, reread that bit if you don't understand. What does that look like? Someone asks you to do something you don't want to do, and instead of making up a long story of excuses you simply say: 'Thank you, no' or simply 'No' and smile. You don't always have to justify yourself, especially when you're protecting something big you're trying to achieve.

There is a kind of reciprocity somewhat like nature offers us in play here: what effort I put in I got a return on. When I jettisoned something I created a space, and as we all know nature hates a vacuum. It got filled instead with an aspect of life I wanted to attract and focus on. This wasn't magical thinking; it was releasing and making space for the new. It was real.

We see this power of release as part of the sacrifice with the mythos of Ix Chel, the fierce jaguar goddess of the ancient Mayan culture. She was the goddess of midwifery, fertility, earth, rain and the sacred sweat bath. Widely honoured, her cult extended at one time as far as the islands off the east coast of the Yucatán Peninsula. However wide her influence, her mythos certainly may once have focused on the practice of the sweat bath, the place where the elderly went to relieve their pain and Mayan mothers went before and after childbirth to ease the process. Birth, rain, pain and sweat baths: all indicate a release of some sort, and it is this wise moon and grandmother goddess who gave wise guidance and protection as a sacrifice of something, in this case labour and maidenhood.

In the Priestess Path we can call upon the releasing powers of goddesses such as Ix Chel when we are ready to let something go. Goddesses such as Kali and Hekate are great for this too, and the phase of the dark moon when it swings around each cycle. Whether it is an excess of anything, bad habit, disease or old patterns, Ix Chel is a powerful discharging force. For those who are getting ready for a birth of something big she is a wise guide and will assist so you have an easier time of it.

TASKS

1. If you get the chance to, go out into the rain for a bit. Imagine the rain washing away your stress and releasing what you don't need.

2. Continue to connect with the moon cycle each night.

3. What would happen if you chose yourself as a priority?

4. What would happen if you chose your own dreams – not being selfish – as a priority for a time?

5. If you choose to be of service to others, how would you balance this in your life so it doesn't become overwhelming?

6. Imagine you have a water jug full of what you would wish to release right now. If you were to tip it all out, what would be released? If you released these things, for your greater good what do you think might happen?

7. What could be birthed instead?

8. Please give some of these new births a timeline.

· MAGICAL WORKINGS ·

Invocation to Odin

Whenever you feel you need good guidance and protection call upon the all-father Odin. You might like to do this invocation on a Wednesday, the day named after him.

Draw Odin's rune symbol, Othala, on a piece of paper. Hold it in your hand and write underneath the symbol where you need guidance specifically, then say:

> *I call you, all-father!*
> *Odin, the seeker, the traveller, the teacher*
> *I seek wisdom and guidance as you once did*
> *Connect me with my own wisdom and*
> *The wise guidance of others*
> *Send your ravens to advise me and*
> *Protect me on my journey to knowing.*

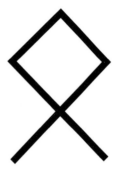

Shut your eyes, relax and allow the form of Odin to come to you. Do not force this. He will come to you in the meditation in a form that you will be happy to accept. Perhaps he will be on his horse, perhaps as a raven or with a wolf at his side. Whatever form he takes he will protect and calm you and give you some indication of what guidance to accept.

When you are ready, open your eyes and record what guidance you have been given. Odin also likes to visit in dreams, so do take note of the dreams you have over the next week or so.

The jar of Ix Chel

This jar should be created on a waning moon cycle or dark moon and prepared beforehand.

You'll need:

* a piece of paper and a pen or some small smooth stones and a texta
* a small jet or obsidian crystal
* a glass jar with lid
* a candle.

Ahead of time, write down on strips of paper or on small stones what you wish to release. Place the jet or obsidian into the jar. On the right moon cycle, go outside and light the candle and say:

> *Ix Chel, I call your name*
> *Woman of the jaguar*
> *Dark as night*
> *I need your help in my own release.*

Hold the paper or stone with the thing/s you wish to release written upon it. Think about how much trouble this thing has been to you and how hard it has been to release it. Allow this emotional energy to rise and put this into the rock. Place the rock or paper into the jar and say:

> *I place this in the jar of Ix Chel to release!*
> *The woman of the jaguar*
> *Dark as night, will hear me*
> *She will change me.*

ANYTHING GREAT REQUIRES A SACRIFICE

Repeat this with each issue you have. Say thank you to Ix Chel when you are done, put the lid on the jar and leave it outside somewhere non-conspicuous under a waning or dark moon. Any time you wish to release something else you can place it in the jar. When the jar is or feels full add water to it, tip the contents out and bury them.

XI

TO DEVELOP COURAGE, BABY, YOU HAVE TO FEEL THE FEAR

Courage is feeling fear but advancing anyway; everyday expressions of courage; the handshake we give to ourselves; the facing of fears; small starts, big finishes; being a hero in our own mythos

The tokoloshe

When I lived in Africa for a bit I would often feel lonely. I was away from home and the culture and people were new to me. Where I lived was remote and at night there were few electric lights and the bush was indeed very dark, so dark that even a grown woman like me would get the spooks sometimes when my room was an absolute vacuum of blackness. Even outside the house, on some nights no stars punctuated the night sky and mother moon hid.

On those nights I often decided to sit and listen to the wise women of the village tell their children bedtime stories as they gathered together in the one room of their home. I was welcomed and was often lulled by their gentle voices speaking the softest Swahili, and as I only understood a little the effect was almost hypnotic in its loving restfulness – that is, until the stories about the tokoloshe.

Tokoloshes are the demons that hide under your bed at night. Yes, really. Many African people are so afraid of tokoloshes that they often traditionally put their bed legs up on rocks or tin cans so that the tokoloshes will have a harder time climbing up into bed with them. What is so bad about these little demons climbing into bed with you? Well, the thing is, tokoloshes strangle you in your sleep unless, of course, you know how to conquer them. But more of that later.

Tokoloshes are very special in their wickedness. They know exactly how to extract the maximum amount of fear in each and every person because they are the embodiment of your worst fear. Just imagine your own personal demon who knows exactly how to scare you into inaction and absolute terror and will strangle any joy, respite and life you may have. The mothers ensured their children also knew that if they had more than one worst fear the tokoloshe would be a combination of all of them!

I sat wide-eyed and sweating just like every other kid in the bedroom when I heard my friends animatedly tell of the horrors of the tokoloshe. I certainly made a detour to the kitchen to get some cans for my bed legs on the way to my bedroom that night. However, there was an upside.

The only way to beat the power of the tokoloshe is to shine a light on it, full on and square. To be able do this, to get the courage up, was so very difficult. This act was very brave because first you had to search for this demon of fear, and second because who knew how ugly and terrifying the tokoloshe actually would be? If you did have the courage to search and find the tokoloshe, if you did shine a light on it to see what it really was, it always lost its power, became very small and ceased to strangle the life from you.

I wonder how many of us have been too afraid to shine a light on our own tokoloshes? I wonder how long we have feared what is hiding under our own beds, how long we have endured the agony of terror and the torture of having no peace of mind? For how long will we allow our fears to strangle the life out of us?

Ah Puch

Ah Puch, the Mayan god of the dead, came out of his underworld home, the nastiest of the nine levels of hell, called 'mitnal'. He stretched his skeletal body and smiled his sharp, white-toothed grin as he began to make his way through the village along the stone pathways.

The Mayan people feared death because of the horrors said to await them should they go to hell, and they were always aware that Ah Puch could indeed be waiting to take them around the next bend. In fact, it is said that at night few people went out on the streets, particularly if there was a sickness within their homes, because Ah Puch may well be stalking them. The people also knew that Ah Puch didn't just come gently for you

TO DEVELOP COURAGE, BABY, YOU HAVE TO FEEL THE FEAR

or would even wait patiently for your death: he hunted for you and he ate your fear. In fact, he gulped it down with relish and was rarely satisfied!

True to form, Ah Puch rattled his skeleton bones and wiggled the bones on his headdress and began to ring his bells. Yes, this most senior of all death demons rang and jiggled all the many bells upon his body so that the people could hear him coming. 'So much more terrifying am I,' thought Ah Puch, 'if the people knew I was around. So much more fearful am I if they can hear me but never dare to confront me. So much more affecting am I if I ring my bells at their doors even if I am not really wanting all of them yet.'

The people knew, however, there was only one way to scare Ah Puch away, and that was to open the doors and scream and shout and sing. Ah Puch lost his power when his bells could not be heard and he was faced and seen, so one night Ah Puch, not heard but faced, slunk back into his underworld home to plan his next visit.

· WALKING THE PATH ·

These two mythos are so similar and rich in meaning yet they come from different continents. Standing strong against any fear – feeling it, shining a light on and confronting it and having the courage to act even when we are scared – is a lesson from both stories we can learn from.

Ah Puch and his fearsome bells always remind me that sometimes my imagination of what could go wrong is far worse than the reality. To me it is far better to act in knowledge rather than wait in worry for fear to hunt you down. I think, also, that sometimes our fears are nebulous, that we don't exactly know what we are afraid of. We hear the bells but don't know specifically what we are fearing, and sometimes this is worse: this hidden nature of our fears if we do not seek them out to look at them.

The idea that the tokoloshe is a bedtime story may alarm some of you, but of course it is ultimately an empowering story used to inspire courage and it has a happy ending. I'm not sure you can teach courage, but we can aspire to it through practice and mindset and certainly inspire it in others. I personally try to name my fears, and this is something we often do to release fear through our magical workings. I have an agreement with myself to confront fears when I can see them and work out whether they are real or ones generated to protect me unnecessarily. This is a kind of handshake with myself that I will shut down what doesn't really advance me or is beneficial to the way I engage with the world and others. It's a kind of spring cleaning of the psyche in a way.

We must, in my view, see our fears as clearly as we can and see them for what they are, often old and limiting.

TASKS

1. What would you do if you had less fear?

2. Name one situation that you think would change for the better if you were more courageous in your handling?

3. What is your greatest fear right now? Is it a real fear or one that is old and outdated and maybe even irrelevant?

4. Make up two lists: fears that have a basis you have control of and fears you don't have control of. I think most people will notice a lot of their fears have a core that they cannot control and, therefore, are useless fears to entertain. Let those ones go and focus on what you can control.

· MAGICAL WORKINGS ·

Shine a torch on fear

We would never summon either of these deities because, well, they are kind of nasty, right? Instead, we ask for courage in our workings. You may wish to confront your fears in this meditation and shine a torch upon it, therefore dispelling it!

You'll need:

* a black candle
* a symbol of your fear
* a torch
* a white candle.

Light the black candle. State what it is you are afraid of and hold the symbol in your hand. Feel the fear emotionally. Take your time. Transfer the feeling of fear by passing the fear from your body to your hands and into the symbol. Place the symbol on the ground in front of you. Pull out the torch, shine the beam directly on the symbol and say:

> *I see you! I see you, my fear*
> *And you are not as terrible as I thought!*
> *I shine light upon you and you reduce!*

Light the white candle, blow out the black one and say:

> *I choose to be courageous and I am not afraid*
> *I step forward fearlessly!*

Bury your symbol of fear in the garden. Allow the white candle to safely burn down.

Building power

Perform this spell on any night where the moon is full or waxing. Decide on the location for the spellcraft, ensuring the space is warm and is a place where you will be undisturbed. Have your intention clearly in mind or written down.

You'll need:

* ✳   a red or black candle
* ✳   sea salt
* ✳   a comfortable robe
* ✳   a piece of paper and a pen or your journal
* ✳   herbs and incense
* ✳   your athame or a blunt knife
* ✳   a symbol of your courage.

Cast and open a circle if you wish. Welcome the goddess and thank her for being with you here tonight in this beautiful place. Light the candle, dim the lights and relax. Take several deep breaths.

Run a bath and add a handful of sea salt, which is very purifying. Soak and relax in the bath for at least 15 minutes. Visualise how good each part of your body feels in that soft, warmth. As you come out of the bath, gently towel off then put on the robe or dress comfortably in something that can be slipped out of easily.

Bring the candle and all of the other equipment into another room or outside if it is warm enough. Face the moon if you can. You can do this spell standing or sitting. Open your power circle. Feel your self-knowledge, self-trust, self-esteem and self-care flood every cell. Breathe in your power.

Ask that you receive the goddess, she who embodies love and courage to bless you this night. If there is a special patron or protective goddess you wish to invoke, do it now.

Look at the candle or close your eyes and go within. State your intention and fear and say:

> *Tonight, I wish to face and conquer my fear*
> *Goddess, my fear is/I am afraid of* [insert your fear statement]
> *I now call forth my fear*
> *Come! Let me see you!*
> *Let me see all that you are!*
> *From beginning to end!*

Look back in your mind and ask to be taken back to the different manifestations of your fear. Allow this to happen in the order that it does; your subconscious will send forth the situations, times and dates. Look to these times in detail and choose one scenario. See this and feel this time clearly in your mind and body. Notice how this fear actually manifests. Is it a feeling? A colour? Where do you feel it or see it first? Feel this fear and its consequences. Allow it to show itself to you. You may now choose to go to the next scenario and repeat this ritual. You should be feeling the effects of your fear.

Ask yourself: what has this fear cost me? What has it stopped me doing, enjoying, discovering? Notice how you feel and what thoughts enter your mind. Record these if you wish.

Light the herbs and incense. Breathe in deeply and, as you breathe in, inhale even more power from the earth, trees, moon and sky. The goddess is still with you and sharing with you. She is with you, standing beside you, assisting you to conquer your fear. You are all powerful. You are goddess/god. Pick up your athame or something you feel you can use as a weapon against your fear and say:

> *I call you fear of* [state what it is]

Show me what you are. Meet me here
Now.

Imagine your fear manifesting into a shape, colour, symbol or creature; this is your fear. You may feel very frightened or you may feel relieved. Perhaps your fear isn't as nasty as you may have first thought now you can see it clearly. No matter, you are ready to be rid of its influence.

First ask your fear: 'What is the positive reason that you are here?' Allow the fear to answer. There will always be a positive intent for a fear no matter what it is. Normally this is a misguided protectiveness. Thank this fear for its positive intent. Tell your fear that you now have the abilities and knowledge to be able to manage it in a better, more healthy way. Tell it that you have no need for the part of it that induces consequences and behaviours such as . . . (insert some of the costs and consequences of having this fear). Tell it that you already know how to do this.

Watch for any changes in the fear: it may accept defeat or it may keep coming. Ask for the goddess and your patron goddess to be with you and state loudly while holding your weapon:

I am warrior. I am goddess. I know who I am and this fear no longer serves me. I let it drop away, die if it be for the good of all and in its place be reborn a better life. The lesson has been learned. I choose another way. Be gone, you are defeated!

Be prepared for your fear to disappear, melt, turn and walk away. On the other hand it may attack you so use your weapon now, being careful to not injure yourself or anything else nearby. You may even use it as a warning. The goddess will assist you in the battle if need be. You will feel her power or the special gifts of your patron goddess. Accept these gifts in your own body and allow these energies to begin to mingle: yours and those of the goddess. Feel your own strength and that of the goddess course through you. You both conquer the fear.

154

In a loud, firm voice say:

> *Be gone, you are defeated!*

As your fear disappears – if it already hasn't – look and feel ahead at what your life will be like now this fear is no longer part of it. Pick up your symbol of courage and chant:

> *I am here again*
> *Change is real*
> *I am free to grow*
> *This is my seal.*

Repeat the chant faster and faster at least three times, feeling your strength, confidence and energy grow. Look to the symbol: this is now your talisman of courage. Keep it as a reminder of how you have conquered this fear. Know that the goddess has assisted you and that she is already helping you find better ways to protect yourself now and into the future.

Thank your patron goddess, and be grateful in the knowledge that all is as you have asked it to be and that your fear has transformed. Know your mind and body are already responding.

Close your circle and your power circle. Take your talisman with you and record your three participatory steps. Extinguish and bury any remaining herbs or incense in the garden or yard. Ground yourself by eating or drinking something, exercising or dancing!

TO DEVELOP COURAGE, BABY, YOU HAVE TO FEEL THE FEAR

XII

YOU WERE NOT MADE TO HIDE: THE GREAT CIRCLE AND THINKING BIG

Forging the new under pressure; leading the way; pulling, not pushing; a season for everything; being seen; the great circle

THE MYTHOS

Éostre

It is said that the goddess Éostre and her hare companion were walking through the land. As she walked, every step brought warmth to the earth. Upon her footfall the ice began to melt, the snow receded and the soil relaxed ready for growth.

Éostre extended her golden energy outwards and sensed a being in need. She came upon a small bird near death in the freezing but melting snow. She held the tiny soul in her hands, trying to revive and warm it but, sadly, its life was too far gone to save. Feeling love and pity for the sweet creature, Éostre transformed the bird back into an egg, giving it a chance to be born again.

Brigid

The first light weakly spilt upon the village. The goddess with flame for hair and who walked with flowers in her footsteps stepped across the land, bringing the rosy light of dawn with her. She passed the forge; it was a special place for her. She made sure that those who created from fire had the power and accuracy to turn liquid metal into objects such as weapons and sacred jewellery. The heat and pressure of the forge, the bringing of the fire of passion, the creation of the new whether art, poetry or metal, all were her domain. She recalls the singing of men long, long ago, their voices lilting. 'Breo-Saighit', she was called, the flame of Ireland.

Glés a hindeón cotad cúar
Clúas a dúan do thengthaib bard
Bruth a fer fri comlann nglan
Cruth a ban fri oenach n-ard.

The ringing of its busy bent anvils
The sound of songs from poets' tongues
The heat of its men at clean contest
The beauty of its women at high assembly
Beannachtaí ar an Ceárta: blessings on the forge!

The people slept, but as she passed their farms she saw homes bowls of spring water and milk and cream and candles that had been left out for her. She touched some of the offerings; she breathed upon others. All had her blessing.

All now that washed with the water would keep their looks and their health until next Imbolc, for she was the essence of healing and new life. All the animals and the land received her blessings too, touched by her power, all returned to warmth and life and robbed by the winter's cold. A great circle of fire with her radiant at the centre touches all but does not burn.

159

· WALKING THE PATH ·

The goddess Brigid, the daughter of the Dagda and one of the poets of Tuatha Dé Danann, is known by many names including Bride (pronounced bri-dee) and Briant. Much loved and actively worshipped, she is the patron goddess of things creative and of healing. She was called upon by smiths of all kinds, writers, musicians, bards and scholars and of course by healers.

The spring festival of Imbolc, which her mythos describes, is still observed by pagans today. It is a time to celebrate the first signs of spring and was considered to be a festival sacred to this goddess. Herbs that were necessary for healing would be gathered and harvested during this time and blessed through ritual in her name. This returning of the light and warmth to the land we see within the beautiful mythos of the Germanic goddess Éostre. The little bird being transformed compassionately into the egg and the featuring of the sacred hare speaks to us of the courage of creation and transformation.

It was also customary to make a Brigid's cross out of straw or sticks. The cross is actually a triskele, which is an ancient symbol of the sun and also reflects the idea of the great circle, the rays pointing out from the middle. The idea of a circle with the energy point radiating out is a potent and poignant one. Circles are an important symbol in paganism and magic. The circle is the shape of our planet and the symbol of unbroken cycles, the sun and the earth. We form protective circles; we send out raised power in spellcraft in circles to the circle of the planet when casting for the healing of the planet. It is an embrace.

Most people would imagine a group of witches in a circle with linked hands sending out their magic together, but it is often a priestess who stands as a conduit in the middle sending out a focused beam of intention to the cause or world. All face her, the energy is raised and is directed to her and she skilfully focuses it on its target. To do this effectively and safely takes skill and practice. It takes trust and humility. It means the priestess is seen both on a mundane and a spiritual level. There is no hiding. You can't be playing small. Big magic means big power.

If we go back to our favourite philosophers, the ancient Greek Stoics, we see they had a series of virtues or values. One was the idea that to be a person of the highest calibre meant that taking care of others in your society was a given. In fact, it was a high duty of being human, a key part of what made you human. This means you had to be involved with others by assisting them or society itself to be better.

We know that archaeologists often measure the sophistication of a society or even whether the humans were of a higher consciousness by whether there is evidence the people looked after others who were less able to survive. For example, if there was evidence of a badly broken leg that had healed over time in a prehistoric skeleton we know that someone had to have fed this person and kept them alive. They didn't leave this human to die but helped them over time to recover.

If we think about the pandemic of COVID-19 we saw how close we all are. Someone sneezed in China and soon the world was doing the same. The pandemic forced us to not be centred just on ourselves but what we could or would be prepared to do to protect others. There was a lot of heated debate. In some places we did that well and in others not so well, and let's not forget the Stoics lived through plague themselves and knew that they had to rely on each other to get through.

To me, if we want to experience big magic and do big things – and going down an alternative leadership pathway like the Priestess Path is a big thing – we must stop playing small and stop hiding. By this I don't mean we need to be totally extroverted and big note ourselves. Nope, not at all. What we do have to do is risk and really commit to a big experience that will, like our goddesses, bring warmth and blessings to our land and for others.

You might think: 'I have no idea what that may be!' There are a couple of emotions we have that can lead us towards what we need or want to experience. When someone tells me they are purposeless or aimless or that they don't have any goals or anything to look forward to, I suggest this simple, rational but profound exercise. I ask them to tell me under what circumstances they feel jealous. I ask them to tell me under what circumstances they feel happy. I ask them to tell me under what circumstances they feel yearning.

Jealousy, happiness and an achy feeling of yearning are emotions that tell us as bright as a bell what we want. Jealousy is simply an emotion that tells us we feel bad for not having something that someone else has. It's useful if we use it as a diagnostic tool, but we have to move through it quickly for it not to be toxic. Happiness is a great feeling emotion and it, too, is a signal for what already makes us content or joyous, so it also clearly guides us forward to things that might give us more of this. Yearning is a deep want for something more profound and shouldn't be ignored. Yearnings for me have always led me to big things, substantial achievements or important associations. Yearnings, whether they are for an experience or place or to do something or be something different. are all keys to growth.

TASKS

1. What inspires you or lights up your passion and what exactly does this feel like for you?

2. What stops you feeling more inspired? Do you ever stop the feeling of inspiration and make yourself small?

3. If it's relevant, why have you stayed small in the past?

4. There comes a time in everyone's life when they have to forge their future. Think of the process of the forge: all that fire, effort and will! What is truly worth it to forge ahead with right now?

5. If you think of the great circle and being connected to all, what would feel big to you?

ᐧ MAGICAL WORKINGS ᐧ

Spell for passion and growth

You'll need:

- ✳ a small spade or large spoon
- ✳ a symbol of what you want to add fertile energy to
- ✳ a few fresh flowers
- ✳ a raw egg still in its shell
- ✳ some native seeds.

Go to your garden, a field or a park: somewhere outdoors that you like. Wear something light that makes you feel good. Dig a small hole in the earth with the spade or spoon and place your symbol in it. The symbol should be something non-toxic that you are happy to leave in the earth. Don't cover it over with dirt. Lay the flowers next to it and say:

> *Blessed Éostre, goddess of spring, bring your energy and your rabbit here! I wish for fertility in . . .* [describe what area it is] *and I wish to join your quickening!*

Hold the egg in your hand. Shut your eyes and imagine the power of the earth and the way it is humming with new life. See grass growing, flowers budding and animals mating and birthing and hear birds singing and insects calling. Feel the air warming. Feel the power of fertility. Boost this feeling by breathing in deeply. Imagine this energy passing into the egg, then open your eyes and say with energy:

> *I call upon the power of spring*
> *The power of green and grow*

> *Éostre, grant me growth*
> *So that I can know and go.*

Crack the egg over the symbol in the hole, which gives fertility to this aspect as you wish. Say:

> *I trust that you, Éostre, have already granted me the power to create.*
> *It has begun!*

Cover the egg and symbol with soil and sprinkle the seeds on top. Give thanks to Éostre. Act upon any ideas you have this day.

Invocation for Brigid

You'll need:

* small amount of rain, well or mineral water
* a large orange candle
* a small white candle
* a small green candle
* a small bowl with a tablespoon full of full cream milk
* a ring or bracelet made of metal.

Dip your hands in the water to cleanse them. Light the orange candle and say:

> *Great Bride, great Brigid, great Breer*
> *I call but a few of your names*
> *Beloved of the smiths, the bards, the scholars, the farmers*
> *I ask that your sacred fires heal me inside and out!*

Light the white candle. Tell Brigid where you need healing and know she is listening. Be as clear and concise as you can but feel free to express your emotions honestly.

Light the green candle and say:

> *Brigid, you heal through the power of the land and from fire. I ask for growth and for healing to begin. I thank you, Brigid, knowing that you will be lighting my way and that profound healing has begun!*

Dip your fingers in the milk and flick some on yourself then say:

> *I take your nourishment and blessings with me.*

Look upon all those candles and at the flames and say:

> *Great Brigid, I claim the fire of creative passion and inspiration for myself.*

Pass the metal piece quickly through the flame for Brigid's blessing. Put it on. Allow the two small candles to burn down then blow out the big candle with thanks. Pour the milk upon the earth. Over the next 28 days, light the big candle for a time each day to receive blessings from Brigid.

XIII

YOUR GREAT WORK

The tradition of the great work; the benefits of greater service; leading by doing; if I can do it, you can too; momentum; worthy sacrifice; legacy; how a great work can circle outwards to something rewarding for you and others

THE MYTHOS

Aradia: mythos one

From she that has always been and he the light bringer, Aradia became flesh and was born upon the earth as a maiden. Her feet bare, her body naked and moonstruck by the silver light of her mother Diana, Aradia's first earthly thought was of love and her second of the connection with all that is. The third, as the first of all the witches known, was to teach the word of her mother and help those who were oppressed and poor.

Knowing that she had a journey ahead, one that might be difficult, she was careful to not reveal entirely who she was at first. As she would spread the word of the feminine divine, in a time when all was changing powerfully towards a god who demanded his masculine self only be loved, she knew of the danger.

She travelled through the countryside and the edges of the burgeoning towns, teaching the women how to hold on to their power, punish oppressors and weave profound magic to heal, to help, to equalise. Through her encounters she learned about hate and intolerance, inequality and equality, shame and pride, death and life and why people were so afraid of their own greatness. She taught. She weaved. She fell in love. She was vulnerable. She faced persecution and was jailed yet she grew into herself, into a powerful feminine force, and she became a model for women into the millennia.

Does it matter whether this story is truth or fiction? Will we ever really know whether Aradia was a flesh and blood woman who was a witch and proud pagan practitioner of the old ways or, indeed, the daughter of a goddess sent to earth? I like to think the lessons of Aradia, her gospel, is mythos in its true defining sense. 'Mythos', a word of Greek origin, means a story with a profound truth. What Aradia brings us is a set of truths valuable to learn from today.

Aradia walked thousands of miles in Diana's service. Meeting in forests, not churches, and fields, not temples, she taught women – young women, widowed women and women with their families – the ways of her mother and of nature. Aradia danced with women, loved them and healed them, and when she began to feel her work would soon be done on earth she hoped the knowledge she had shared would continue without her. She hoped that through her work her message would survive.

However, one night, Aradia and a gathering of night women were singing and dancing in a forest clearing under the bright moonlight when a woman Aradia had never seen before walked by. Catching sight of the ceremony, the woman screamed in outrage at what she saw as witches undertaking the work of the devil. She told Aradia that she would call for soldiers and that Aradia and the other women would all be arrested.

While some of the women were terrified, knowing such an occurrence would bring great shame to their families – and even put them at enormous physical risk – some were defiant, happy that at last their faith would be revealed for all to see but Aradia understood there was an even greater danger. She knew she had to protect these women because they were to be the custodians of her message of the feminine divine. If they and their knowledge were lost, all of her life's work would be lost with them.

Instead, she told the angry woman that the gathered women were under her spell, and that their behaviour that night was not their fault. In this way Aradia was able to convince the stranger to arrest her and her alone. Before Aradia sent the night women back to their homes she swore them to secrecy and asked them to vow that no matter what happened they would protect what they had learned from her and pass it only to those of blood or whom they knew would not betray them.

Soon the soldiers arrived to take Aradia away. As they led her across a wide swathe of the strange woman's land Aradia learned it was royal land and that the woman who had discovered her was the king's sister.

The woman, whom Aradia now knew was a princess, caused Aradia to be locked away in a tall stone tower.

Aradia felt afraid, for she had seen the horrors that some humans had visited upon one another. With only a strand of moonlight for company, she prayed to her mother. As the silver light of the moon played upon her beautiful form, Aradia sang songs of devotion to Diana. Her voice was so pure that as she sang a nightingale began to harmonise with her. Gracefully, she swayed to the rhythm of the words and at last, feeling stronger and less vulnerable, she became certain that all would be for her greatest good.

Unbeknown to her, the king himself had come to see the haughty witch his sister discovered in the forest. He came with both anger and curiosity. He had heard of witches but had never seen one, and he expected to find something out of a nightmare. He was very wrong. Stopped in his tracks at the sight and sound of Aradia, he dropped silently to his knees to witness her communion with Diana. First he saw her fears and tears, and then her beauty and grace. Finally, the king heard the goodness and purity of her songs. How could this be evil? he wondered. How could what he saw be the work of a demon?

Every night for three nights the king secretly watched Aradia and found himself entranced by her. On the third night he introduced himself and declared his love. Aradia, surprised to find she had been watched, was even more stunned to realise that she felt a connection with the king. How could this be, when he was a king and of a Christian path and she was the daughter of a goddess and of a very different path?

The young king granted Aradia her freedom and then asked her to be his wife, his queen. While she felt she loved this man, Aradia was worried that such a marriage would be confining and would require her to obey her king before her mother, Diana. Uncertain of what to do, Aradia returned to the forest, where she made her way through the huge roots of an ancient tree and found a hiding place underground. There, as she contemplated her way forward, she had a vision in which she witnessed the meeting of two halves of a tree. Aradia interpreted this as representing her marriage to the king and saw that not only would it be one of honour and love, but it could also synergistically join the old and new ways together. Her marriage could be a way to bring the masculine and feminine together in greater equality. It could bring the hierarchy to a centre point for the benefit of all. Her marriage could bring relief to communities that were struggling under the yolk of poverty and tyranny.

Upon her return from the deep earth Aradia spoke eloquently to her suitor, telling him of her vision and all she felt it could mean for the people of his realm. The king saw the wisdom in Aradia's words. If she would join him as his queen, he agreed to endeavour to create the balance in his kingdom that she spoke of, a balance that would allow the best of both worlds to exist.

While Aradia and the king were both delighted with the promise their anticipated marriage held, the king's sister was not happy at all. She told the king he had been bewitched, and that his betrothed was evil. Aradia learned of the princess's lies and that the princess had a beloved son who was dying from a fever. Despite the cruelty she had experienced at the princess's hands, Aradia healed the young prince when medicine men and priests could not. Now grateful, the princess embraced Aradia and they became as sisters.

It was said that Queen Aradia taught the old ways while the king honoured the new. Their kingdom, thus balanced, was the most prosperous in Italy.

Prometheus

Prometheus, the son of the Titan Iapetus, was asked by Zeus to create man. After deftly forming men from water and earth, the humans who were formed by sacred clay were fashioned in the god's image, unlike other animals. These new beings became beloved by Prometheus even though it seemed they had no fur for warmth, no great teeth for protection, were short lived and possessed few skills to help them survive well.

Feeling pity for his magnificent creations, Prometheus decided to help them although he knew to do so would bring down upon him the wrath of the king of all gods, Zeus. Already in trouble for his foresight in tricking Zeus into accepting a different – and in Zeus's eyes lesser – way of men honouring and sacrificing to him, Prometheus could at first only watch as Zeus took the vital gift of fire from mankind.

Prometheus knew that fire would allow men to grow and thrive and was necessary to their survival. He knew that all art and skills such as metal-making would only blossom with fire, so he crept into Zeus's own hearth and, lighting a small flame within a stalk of giant fennel, took the fire and escaped the notice of Zeus.

But not for long . . .

Zeus instructed Hephaistos (Vulcan) to fashion woman – yes, as a negative distraction for man! – and to rivet the body of Prometheus to a mountain. Here a great eagle would pick at Prometheus's liver until sunset every day, whereupon the organ would magically regrow overnight so he could relive the same agony each new day for eternity. Happily, the hero Herakles eventually slew the eagle and freed Prometheus.

Today we know how important altruism is, especially in a world that has grown as unequal as ours has. In a time of climate change and a bigger gap between rich and poor than ever, acting on behalf of the greater good and not just our individual selves will not only be an ethical act but soon one of survival.

The bowl of light (Hawaii)

It is believed that each of us is born to the planet with a bowl of light and made of light that is connected with the source, where all has come from.

This bowl is perfect and shines brightly, and each bowl represents the truth and essence of that particular person.

It is the parents' and guardians' job at first to help a child retain and grow their light. They should teach them how to respect the light they have and to have love run through all things. If this is done well and the child is guided to their potential they will grow from strength to strength, their light not dimming, and their health will flourish. They will be aligned with all others, too, full of love and compassion and in balance with nature. They can swim like fishes, hunt with sharks, play like a turtle, fly like a bird, be warm like the sun.

Yet if this child experiences hate and that life is not of love then things will be different. If the child experiences great fear, self-hatred or shame then they place a dark stone into the bowl. Some of the light is blocked. When enough stones fall in the light is dimmed. If there is too much darkness there is no room for the light to shine at all and, of course, there are stones in that bowl. Stones are heavy. Stones are hard to carry. And stones can be stagnant.

There is a way for the bowl to be light again: by rejecting the stones, by turning the bowl upside down and allowing the stones to be tipped out. Through tipping them out, looking at them but not picking them up again, the light can be returned.

· WALKING THE PATH ·

There is a tradition within many witchcraft pathways that involves a commitment of service to the wider community through an active project. This project can be a one-off or ongoing – many end up being catalysts for big things – but it has to be a project that is undertaken over time and involves some difficulty and challenge. We call this a 'great work'.

What a great work is not is a quick donation to your favourite charity and it isn't organising something to get yourself a job or earn money for yourself. although indirectly that could occur. It is something that is for the benefit of many others, not just your kids or family. A great work is a gift to your community, your society or the world. It may even be the stuff of a legacy for yourself. While it may feel big and scary for you to consider it you should feel lit up by it. If you achieved it, it would be something important to you and others. If you shut your eyes right now you could imagine yourself completing it and the positive impact it would have. Traditionally, the time to get that great work completed or very much underway was a year, one cycle of the earth around the sun.

When I was challenged with the idea of a great work it filled me with both terror and enthusiasm. I have never been someone short of ideas, but this had to be something that wasn't really aimed at me. Instead, it was aimed at the greater good. What would this be? How would I do this? How would I find the time with everything else I had going on?

The short answer was to look for the passions I had and, strangely enough, the things that made me a bit angry or for which I felt justice wasn't being done. Things that I felt needed to change guided me, and if this project was going to be one that meant a sacrifice in my time and effort then I had to really feel pulled to do it. There had to be, at its heart, something that hit my values, virtues, talents and joys.

After much soul searching I decided to write my first book, one based on witchcraft. I wanted it to be more mainstream than most. Remember that this was more than 20 years ago. I wanted it to be a demystifying and modern book on how to have business success through the power of this pagan path. I had never written a book before. Sure, I was a writer as part of my job, but a book wasn't on my list of things I had considered. It is perhaps pertinent to admit that I wasn't out of the broom closet, that most people, including my family and workplace, had no idea I was a witch and pagan.

The stakes felt high but, challenged the priestess who trained me, what if 'this book helped pagans and non-pagans to do business with more integrity, joy, attraction and kindness and that they get introduced to another way of doing things rather than the patriarchal way? What if it helped a lot of people? What if it inspired young women in particular to be led by both logos and mythos?'

Well, that might be worth doing it for, right?

I planned out what I wanted to write. I gave myself a structure and a timeframe, which blew out almost immediately. Every time I faltered, every time I had self-doubt, my mentor reminded me why I was doing it. This wasn't for me; I was doing this to serve. After a couple of years I completed the book and the first publisher I sent it to took it on. As it covered quite an usual topic in an unusual way, media got on to it. The leading financial magazine at the time, *Money Magazine*, gave it 5 out of 5 stars but with the comment 'I wanted to hate this book, but the author, "a witch", made so much sense I couldn't.'

Hundreds of people wrote to me about how the book opened something different for them in the way they saw prosperity or ran their businesses, and there isn't a public event I go to where someone doesn't tell me this book was their first exposure to modern paganism and it encouraged them to seek more. There was also an unexpected benefit: it created the momentum for me to serve more. It was the conduit to more writing and more teaching. It enabled me to step into a self-supporting role in which I could enact more of my work as a priestess. I could write, teach, engage, speak and ultimately serve the community full time. I got to empty the rocks out of my bowl of light once more.

Here we are near the end of the 13 lessons. We may, in fact, have been working together for 13 moons or more. You won't be the same person

who started this book. Hopefully you're surer of yourself, stronger, more secure, more creative, more joyous and radiating calm and passion in equal rays! Now I'm asking you to put yourself out there, be courageous and do something that is big for the greater good. Maybe you'll be a priestess.

Examples of great works that I have been close to include:

* Obtaining funding for a women's refuge. A lot of money raised.
* The founding of a breed-specific dog refuge.
* An annual art fund-raiser for young artists who cannot afford materials or books for their study and work.
* An indigenous language centre.
* Organising a chain of community gardens and teaching people how to grow their own food.
* Someone deciding they'd had enough of politicians doing corrupt things in their area and running for local council. They won.
* Someone donated a piece of land to be rewilded in their area and oversaw the vast amount of expert work to do this.
* The production of a short film about sharks and why they are a valuable part of the ecosystem.
* The establishment of a work clothing library for women who don't have suitable clothes for job interviews.

So how about it?

I want to hear from you. If you are in fact attempting a great work I want to know! I want to support you. Go to my website themodernwitch.com and contact me through there, and if you wish I'll connect you with others of your ilk. If you are supporting the greater good I want to support you.

TASKS

1. Get a pack of Post-it notes and write down everything that lights you up about the great work and stick them on a wall.

2. Write down on the Post-it notes what your greatest passions are for the planet and for the beings of the planet.

3. Write down the biggest problems in your community you think need to be solved.

· MAGICAL WORKINGS ·

I thought as well as giving you a beautiful invocation to bring you towards your great work I would add in some ritual notes on the kind of rites we typically do as priestesses after completing our great work should we choose to be fully initiated within our tradition.

Enjoy.

Courage with Prometheus

Light a candle or build a small fire. If you're burning a candle, anoint it with fennel oil prior to burning it or throw a handful of resin incense into the flames to fragrance them. Say:

> *I honour your gift, Prometheus.*

Next, say:

> *I call you, son of Iapetus*
> *You who thought only of the greater good and not of himself*
> *You who made man in the image of the gods from sacred clay*
> *It is a rare gift of skill that does not come from you.*
> *Your talent, your foresight, your love of others*
> *Is something that I wish to emulate*
> *I call you, Prometheus*
> *Mould me, just as you did in the beginning*
> *Free me from constraint and allow me to teach and work on behalf of others*
> *Allow me to think of the greater good and not just of myself.*
> *Show me how to think strategically for the greatest impact*
> *To use my unique gifts for the best ends*

> *With all my heart I ask to be gifted of your bravery and courage*
> *In your name for the good of all*
> *In gratitude, I trust all will be as I have asked.*

Leave the candle until it burns down.

Witches and priestesses were always considered to be the wise ones of the village. They could be relied upon for healing and good counsel. Very few leaders in ancient times made major decisions without first consulting the wise of their country or those who were able to translate oracles. Oracles such as that at Delphi were famous for hundreds of years and gave guidance to kings and those who would be kings.

Our problem, of course, was to find ways to continue or evolve our traditions during the long periods of persecution. Happily, attitudes have changed somewhat and there is a noticeable resurgence in bringing back some of the old traditions and celebrations, especially those that mark significant moments in our personal timeline. Witches believe the sharing of wisdom is one of the most enduring ways to connect and reconnect with those closest to us and to the wider world. Most of the ways we choose to share our traditions involve education or celebrations or both.

TRADITIONAL/ MODERN CEREMONIES

As the cycle of the seasons and the balance of light and dark changes so do the stages of our lives. You don't have to be a witch or pagan to put one of these great ceremonies together. Pagans really know how to celebrate, so why not join in the fun?

BIRTHS

As the goddess is a creative force, the birth of a baby is celebrated with great joy by witches. Witches were often the midwives of a community and brought many children into the world through their birthing skills and spiritual remedies. In my temple tradition one of the things we do is sing the baby out, filling both mother and baby with hope and encouragement. The priestess is often the first non-family member to handle the child.

As the Christian faith has rituals, namely christenings, that welcome and initiate babies into the family of their god, wicca has wiccanings. Many wiccans, though, prefer to allow the child to choose what faith they are when they are old enough to do so instead of initiating them at their personal choice. As such these parents choose wiccan blessings or simple spiritual ceremonies that ask the community to join together to guide and bless their child. I have included below a simple ceremony with exactly this intention. Enjoy!

BABY BLESSING CEREMONY

Ahead of time invite your friends to think of a non-material gift for the child. This gift should be represented in some symbolic way; for example, the last gift I gave was the gift of a great sense of humour. I represented this with a little card with a montage on it of things that make me laugh. The friend who accompanied me gave the gift of integrity represented by a white feather, which is the symbol of Ma'at, the goddess of truth and justice.

On the day of the baby blessing ceremony three candles should be lit: one for the goddess, one for the child and one for the life they will co-create together. The child should be held by the parents and a bowl held by the god or goddess parents to hold all the gifts. One by one guests come forward and offer their gift to the baby and the parents accept the gift on the child's behalf. The gifts should then be catalogued in the family book of shadows, and items may be kept or photographed.

Each guest is given a small token gift of thanks from the baby. This may be a simple flower, seed or the baby's footprint on a card.

FIRST MOONTIME

One of the most rewarding things about being a witch community is that I am often invited to take part in various ceremonies that mark special times in the lives around me. Pagan traditions, like many others throughout the world, welcome the transition between various ages. For example, in the Jewish faith when a boy reaches the age of manhood at 13 he is welcomed into manhood through his bar mitzvah. For girls the ceremony is a bat mitzvah. In many goddess traditions such as wicca, the time a girl experiences her first moon bleed is marked and honoured. I have been to a number of these ceremonies, and they are incredibly empowering and life affirming for the young woman.

I remember as a young girl how confusing the whole menstrual thing was. There was no celebration as such and a lot of uncertainty and fear around the pain. I was lucky in that there was little shame attached to my moon bleed experience, but for the majority of women there is.

The idea that this blood is dirty and undesirable has been propagated by many societies and cultures, and the belief that the bleed makes us unhealthy or weak is still a popular one. In contrast, within many goddess religions menstrual blood is considered to be a highly magical substance, and permeating all is the knowledge that a woman's moontime is a perfectly natural and powerful one. I believe it is every woman's duty to encourage the young to see how intrinsically special our moon blood is and to celebrate its presence rather than teaching young people it is something to be avoided or dreaded.

GIRLS' MOONTIME CELEBRATIONS

To celebrate a first moon bleed you may wish to have a special women-only celebration. Perhaps it's a very special dinner in a good restaurant

or beautiful hotel or an overnight stay in nature. The important thing, though, is the company. The girl is now a woman and should see that she can share in the glories of womanhood.

Allow her to hear and be a part of great conversation and have answer any of her questions about womanhood. You may want to give her a piece of good jewellery to mark the occasion that you have blessed with moon water. When she is old enough she may wish to pass this jewellery on to a young woman at her first bleed, and thus pass on the wisdom. Take your daughter or the young woman to a bookstore and buy her a number of books you believe show the world in its infinite variety and humans at their most creative. These books may be the start of the young woman's getting of wisdom. Introduce the idea of lunar returns to her and explain her special moon.

I would also advise bringing up your boys to appreciate the magical differences between the sexes and discussing the moon cycles with them. Boys who are brought up with an honour for the feminine and a strong appreciation for their own strengths as being masculine are often more balanced and empathetic men.

HANDFASTING

Handfasting is the term given to traditional pagan wedding ceremonies. Originally, the two partners were joined for a period of one year and agreed to be faithful to one another for this time – no other hands but theirs – after which they would be free to decide whether they wished to be joined ever after. Sometimes the ceremony involved the jumping of the couple over the woman's broom, which signified the joining of the two homes. There is evidence of other actions such as tying hands together with a beautiful fabric woven by the family or even the feeding of blessed food to the couple so they were joined body and soul.

Today, many pagan folk like to combine some of the rituals of handfasting into a marriage sanctioned by law. There are pagan celebrants who can legally marry couples through handfasting ceremonies in most countries, or you could write your own ceremony and ask a civil marriage celebrant to incorporate it into the legal requirements. I have a number of handfasting ceremonies on my website should you be interested in utilising them in detail, although the elements they have in common are as follows:

* There is a celebration of the uniqueness of the individuals, which gives a highly personalised quality to the ceremony.
* There is a dedication of freedom of expression during the marriage yet of harm none.
* There is equal time given to the male and female energies, and a chalice and athame are often used to symbolise this.
* Promises are made by the couple to each other that are valid as long as their love lasts.

Although there is some binding symbology such as joining of hands with fabric or drinking from a common chalice of wine, the couple are reminded that they will always be individuals and should grow strong together by being apart.

CRONING

Our youth-obsessed Western culture has little time or honour for age. Age truly is a dark taboo and one in which women are particular victims. In pagan societies all ages were honoured for different reasons, but it was those who had the life experience to gather and grow wisdom that were most venerated. These were the people a person could learn skills and take counsel from and even take sanctuary with. The most powerful witches in such societies were naturally the older women, the crones or elder women of the area. Once these women reached a certain age, normally around 60 or when their menstrual blood ceased to flow completely, a special ceremony would take place called a 'croning'.

The croning ceremony would celebrate their abundance of wisdom now that their moon blood was kept within them. These women were particularly skilled and powerful and therefore the most dangerous to the new religion. The idea of the ugly, old crone as the evil witch was

an easy leap to make for the storytellers of the new ways. Unfortunately, the word 'crone' became something no woman would want to be labelled with, and the idea of venerating such a creature fell away – until perhaps the last 20 or so years. Here is what three women had to say about their own modern cronings:

* 'I felt honoured and exhilarated to be the age that I am.' Eda, 60, USA
* 'I must say I was feeling quite unconfident before the croning. Worse, I was feeling invisible. The croning clearly made me see again what I had to offer, and it was plenty!' Susan, 62, Australia
* 'This was one of the best days of my life. So many amazing women there and they honoured me by asking me to share my wisdom. It left me feeling very vital and useful.' Abbey, 72, Australia

There are as many ways to celebrate a croning as there are ways to cook eggs, but allow me to share a format I like.

Croning celebration framework

You can hold a croning for yourself or for someone else. Choose a great outdoor venue and put aside at least one whole day. Some of the best cronings I have been to have been a weekend away in nature, but if time does not permit a day will do. The venue should be private enough that you will not be disturbed and open enough that it gives you some room.

Invite all age groups. The more generations the better! Choose a facilitator or priestess to run the show. They need not be witches, but they should certainly understand the core themes of what you are doing. Prepare a feast of the crone's favoured foods and a decorated chair to act as a throne for your crone. Everyone should decorate this using flowers, tinsel or whatever you like.

When the time comes, play the crone's favourite music and carry the throne into the centre of the space you are using. Dance around and sing along with the music. Bang drums if you have them. Place the decorated chair in the centre of the circle and call in your crone. Give her a huge round of applause and cheer as she sits in the centre of you all on that amazing chair. Light one candle for her, one for the goddess and one for the combined wisdom.

Your facilitator will then explain the process to all present and allow everyone to speak in turn and share stories of wisdom and love for the crone. They may even have pictures or objects as evidence for her good deeds and great wisdom. The crone will then talk about her like and speak to each person individually, commenting on their words and sharing a piece of wisdom especially for them. She will next open the floor to questions and problems. The circle normally throws up some current vexing problems, and whether they are about love, relationships, children, spirituality or work, the crone will pass on her wisdom and call on others to assist if necessary.

I have never been to a croning where there isn't a belly laugh, many tears and some amazing wisdom passed on. Someone may also like to make a record of what is said or take photographs.

The circle is closed when everyone is ready by offering a glass of fine wine or champagne to each, a final intention with much applause and dancing!

THE WHEEL
OF THE YEAR

As well as working through the 13 lessons, as I mentioned earlier in the book you might also wish to begin a seasonal practice of your own that is beneficial in mind, body and spirit. Importantly, these sacred times will connect you with the light, land and seasons. The land is our mother; she feeds us, shelters us and gives us comfort and joy. The festivals of the wheel of the year offer a chance to give something back to her and honour all that she does. As modern people we often forget this and feel disconnected without quite knowing why.

The continuous cycle lends itself to the image of a wheel always turning, always progressing. The ancient Celts and their predecessors saw time as a wheel or spiral divided by eight festivals as outlined below. Modern witches can use the themes of each celebration to do magical workings of their own in complete synergy with the natural cycles. The dates featured on solstices and equinoxes are a guide only, so please refer to local astronomical calendars for solstice and equinox timings for accuracy. Better still, get yourself a *Lunar & Seasonal Diary* for your hemisphere to keep you up to date – I've got an annual one that I've been producing for almost 20 years. See the modernwitch.com for details.

SAMHAIN

SOUTHERN HEMISPHERE 30 APRIL–1 MAY
NORTHERN HEMISPHERE 31 OCTOBER

Happy witches' New Year! Samhain or Halloween is considered to be the beginning of the witches' year, but isn't Halloween about death? How can that Sabbath be something that signals a beginning? Because witches see death – the void – as the beginning of life, so Samhain is our special time.

In ancient agricultural times fallow fields indicated the beginning of the preparation for life. We see Samhain like a fallow field: it might look empty with nothing growing, but in reality that isn't true. Fallow fields aren't empty; they are waiting, resting and restoring iand are receptive. Most of all, they are full of potential and possibility. That, to me, is the whole idea of celebrating a new year: starting from a position of total possibility. It's a joyful place, is it not?

Death then becomes the theme of this holiday in its most positive terms. Death can signal our ability to start again, and thus becomes a part of life and the step before renewal. Having a celebration about death, treating it lightly and with laughter, helps us see that there is little to be afraid of and it helps our society lift this last taboo.

Halloween or All Hallows Eve is traditionally a winter festival marking the colder time and a time when the earth begins to retreat and die. It is traditionally the time when it is said the wall between the spirit world and our world is at its thinnest, which gives us a good opportunity to honour our friends and ancestors who have passed over in fun and loving ways.

While it may sound confusing, pagans in the southern hemisphere do not celebrate Halloween on 31 October. Why? It's not the right time seasonally!

As the season here is far from winter, instead they celebrate the opposite seasonal festival of Beltane, a spring celebration of creation and fertility. It is more correct in the southern hemisphere to celebrate Halloween on 30 April, when Beltane is celebrated in the northern hemisphere.

HOW TO CELEBRATE SAMHAIN

Everyone knows about the idea of trick or treating but it is not the only way to celebrate this festival. I very much enjoy having a Samhain feast in which I decorate the table beautifully and have others of like mind around. I always set a place at the table at Halloween dinner for those who have passed, and we all talk about them with love and tell tall and wonderful stories about them. Sometimes people bring pictures of those who have passed or an object they owned. It certainly isn't a time for sadness but is a time to celebrate that we knew them.

The thinness is also why many people from all over the world on this night choose to use a variety of divination tools and methods to get a glimpse of their future or to tap into some wise messages from the other side. Why not try this simple form of divination before dinner? Put some water and ice in a long transparent glass. Have a candle or light source close to the glass so that it lights up. Gather round the glass so you all can see it. Drop food colouring or indigo ink into the glass and, as the ink drops and makes patterns, allow your intuition to see and identify symbols and pictures in the glass. Take note of these and record them, as these are often messages sent from the other side. Why not action them as soon as possible?

YULE
WINTER SOLSTICE

SOUTHERN HEMISPHERE 21–23 JUNE
NORTHERN HEMISPHERE 21–23 DECEMBER

For the ancient people living on the land summer and autumn meant hunting and harvest aplenty, but with the coming of winter life was more often challenging. Traditionally, winter's bareness brought with it a leaner, more difficult time and often the end of a life cycle, a figurative or literal death, so for many surviving this harsh part of the winter was a big achievement!

The idea that after this longest of nights light and warmth would again be returning was a cause for celebration. This fire festival came to be called 'Yule'. It was naturally a time for hope and a celebration of the light returning. A large tree was cut down, a log taken to burn and the rest of the tree brought inside to signify the return of warmer, greener times. And, yes, it became widely appropriated by Christians and some of its traditions made it into what we now know as Christmas.

HOW TO CELEBRATE YULE

Every year my family creates a Yule log. It's normally a log cut from one of the branches that seem always to fall from our tree in the winter storms around my home. We have an open fire, but a campfire or fire in a fire pit is just as good. I love the idea that people have been making and burning Yule logs for a very long time. Once you have your log, write your wishes and hopes on little bits of coloured paper and pin them to the log, then add the log ceremonially to your roaring fire. Give a cheer and a hearty toast to it all coming true!

In its ancient form Yule is a solar festival in which traditionally all lights and fires were put out and a new one lit at midnight to symbolise a fresh start, then from that first fire all the rest were lit. Yule also naturally involves a feast – wintery foods are served – and the table is decorated with a centrepiece of blazing gold, red and green candles. The traditional drink is spiced, warmed mulled wine or warmed honey cider.

Traditionally, too, Yule is a good time to make charms and talismans for abundance. Present giving is also usual, but wherever possible the presents should be home made.

IMBOLC
A CELEBRATION OF THE LIGHT RETURNING

The festival of Imbolc is a celebration centred around the warmth and sun returning to the land. Originally it was a celebration particularly honouring the goddess Brigid in her fiery spring aspect. It was a time when the lambs were born and plants began to awaken. It's the perfect time to ask for clarity of purpose and an increase self-knowledge, so allowing your true light to shine.

Look about you: there would be some hints in your environment that the earth has begun to change and wake up as Brigid's fire warms the land. It is now time to awaken ourselves too. Shake it off and invite in all manner of growth, creativity and love. It's the childhood of the god.

HOW TO CELEBRATE IMBOLC

During Imbolc you may wish to add some special presents for Brigid to your celebration, perhaps some cakes baked in her honour or a special candle, bigger than the rest, that you light to remember her. Traditionally, a mass of white candles is lit upon altars and a lit candle can be carried from room to room of the house to welcome the sun and celebrate its growing strength.

Below is one of my favourite invocations for Brigid. If you are looking to add some fire to your life because you are feeling passionless or purposeless or lack inspiration of any kind, try this invocation at any time during the waxing moon this month. Say:

> *Great Bride, I have lost my fire, bring it back to me*
> *Great Bride, I have found my passion, grow it like a tree*
> *Great Bride, I forge my purpose, like metal in a flame*
> *Let me step in confidence, let me dance your name.*

You might also collect the goddess Brigid's healing waters from your garden for potion making and spellcasting. To do this, collecting the dew on Imbolc morning by leaving out a bowl with a small amount of water the night before. It is said that if you rub the water on your face on Imbolc morning you won't age another year!

OSTARA
SPRING EQUINOX

This is the other equinox (equal time) of the year, when the hours of night and day are equal although from tomorrow the days grow longer. This means that the warmth and light are returning to the earth hour by hour, day by day. It is a beautiful time of joy and balance! Our ancestors would have been planting and counting all the livestock that would have been born by now and gaining weight. Nature has her powerful growing energy on and we should flow with this and not against it.

Ostara is the time to look again at how balance is playing out in your life and how you can set new intentions to find more of it. This equinox also leads us into longer hours of sunlight and therefore more growth as we move towards the ripeness of summer. This is not the time to stand still.

Ostara celebrates the inherent fertility in all of us and our birthright of divine creation. It is a perfect time to begin something new, to let go of the old that isn't working for you and rejoice in the sheer wonder of a fresh start. Again, this spring festival is one of the mind and body, and health and nourishment play a part. Kicking old bad habits to the curb is perfect timing. It's about now, too, that we begin to get the urge to have a good spring clean of our home, work and psyche.

All kinds of spring deities are honoured at this time such as Éostre, Cernunnos, Freya, Hebe, Persephone, Blodeuwedd and so on.

197

HOW TO CELEBRATE OSTARA

The timing of Ostara lends itself to the setting of intentions for bodily and life balance. If you wish to balance your body to achieve, for example, less stress or better immunity, this is a powerful time of year to do it.

Decorate your altar with flowers and honey and the brighter colours of spring. Ditch your winter colours and try to get up a little earlier to catch the first light and greet the dawn. Eggs are a powerful symbol of Ostara, most probably linked with the the Germanic goddess Éostre, so they are wonderful to use in ritual. Plant seeds in your garden but do them mindfully with a little wish upon each one. Dig your holes, hold the seed and wish upon it, then breathe gently upon it and plant it with love and care. Water the seed afterwards. Know that as these plants grow so do your wishes!

THE SENSUAL SPRING RITUAL

Let's get our bodies back into it for spring with this ritual. Gather some fresh flower petals, a variety of native seeds, at least seven coins of any denomination and a small green candle. Put the petals, seeds and coins in a small bag and step outside and go for a walk. It matters not where; just begin to walk. As you go, concentrate on the feeling of the air on your skin and the sunlight or rain as well. Be aware of the birds and the sound of the trees. Look around you: absorb the colours of the sky, the ground, the flowers – everything – as you walk. Take a deep breath. What do you smell? Pollen? Moisture? Grass?

Feel how good it feels to be so connected to the energies of nature during Ostara. Smile! Put your hand in the bag and pull out a pinch of what's inside – it could be a coin and some petals or seeds and some herbs – and sprinkle them as you walk. If you are on a footpath make sure you sprinkle on the nature strip. Avoid cement if you can. As you sprinkle say:

> *Wake up! Wake up! A gift for you!*

After a time, repeat this and continue until there is nothing left in the bag. Go home, light the green candle and say:

> *Gods and goddesses of spring, may all receive your blessings and be expanded. May I begin . . .* [tell them what you wish to begin]. *May I let go of . . .* [tell them what you want to let go of]. *Thank you!*

Let the candle safely burn down.

BELTANE
(BEL TAN, BELTAINE)

This festival is the direct opposite on the wheel of the year to Samhain. As Samhain is related to death, Beltane is related to conception and life. It is a celebration that calls for a little wildness and a lot of joy! The original Beltane celebrations called for the May queen and king of the community to be joined together, and after ritual they would make love. The people of the land would be happy to show their appreciation on their own land later by feasting, running and also doing what comes naturally at springtime! If you have ever seen a maypole, which is often the centrepiece of the celebrations of May Day, perhaps you can guess why it is shaped the way it is!

It is also a perfect time to take stock of what you want to invest yourself in for the future, to rededicate yourself to a healthy body, clear and happy mind and a deep and flowful spirit. Along with autumn, spring is a traditional time for retreats because of this sacred period of transition being held as such a vital way to bring additional positive power and direction to life.

HOW TO CELEBRATE BELTANE

Community festivals and maypoles were the traditional way of celebrating Beltane. Instead of a traditional maypole, try decorating a tree in your backyard with red and white ribbons in celebration or wrap ribbons around your broom and display it in a prominent place. You might invite your friends over for an outdoor barbecue or to a party with a bonfire on the beach.

The other more ancient way to celebrate was a Beltane run; however, I understand that isn't for everybody! Instead, you might even paint up your body with pretty symbols – gold body paint is perfect – and take a run around your garden or dance happily to some music at home to raise your energy. The thing is to celebrate the most fertile of festivals energies by allowing yourself a little wildness and merry making. It is a magical night for lovers and lovemaking, so do take that into account.

I clear off my altar completely and redecorate it with fresh flowers, spring fruits and light green candles. I also make love and health potions on this day as the energy is very strong in these areas. If you are casting, spells for friendship, love, conception, creativity and prosperity are appropriate at this time.

LITHA
SUMMER SOLSTICE

SOUTHERN HEMISPHERE 21–23 DECEMBER
NORTHERN HEMISPHERE 21–23 JUNE

If summer is the peak seasonal energy, Litha is the peak of the peak! Litha celebrates the longest day and the shortest night in the year, so we are marking the most powerful of solar energies. It is traditionally the time when the masculine divine is at its strongest, and it is on this day that we take the time to honour the gods in our practice.

At the centre of Litha is the energy of gratitude and being aware of the importance and power of the present. We also appreciate what we have been able to bring to fruition with our hard work and energy throughout the year. This is important stuff: we often just push on, not acknowledging how far we have come and what we have achieved, and wonder why we get disgruntled or weary. Honour what you have done positively for yourself and also honour the things that maybe haven't worked out. Why? Because if you can see these as information to do it better next time you have reason to celebrate!

HOW TO CELEBRATE LITHA

I set my alarm for just before dawn and light a big gold or orange candle as the light begins to break over the horizon. I offer my gratitude to the seasonal energies and for being able to soak up all that vibrational energy of fruition. I then ensure I plug in to the earth by breathing deeply and allowing my energy to travel downwards through my feet and then pulling up the energy from the earth into my body – right up to the top of my head.

Every single cell gets to experience that powerful solar energy of fruition and lushness!

Being a solar festival, the most powerful time to honour the masculine divine is at midday when the solar energies are at their peak. I do a small ritual thanking the masculine divine for the continual love and protection I receive. Practically, I leave out a large bowl of water for an hour or two from midday to make solar water. This water is wonderful for charging up crystals or blessing areas for protection. I also like to use it in baths for health and vitality.

Litha is also a time when we ask for and share in prosperity of all kinds. Spells for increasing our prosperity, whether that is cash flow, more remuneration or an increase in clients are very powerful at this time. Charging up talismans for this reason could have no more potent a day than this one.

How to celebrate Mabon:

Like Lammas, Mabon is a time to recognise the harvest of your life and to be grateful for what we have. That could be something very simple – that we have food to eat, we are alive and healthy, that we see a beautiful flower on the way to work or a cute dog on the street. As such I always try and cook something special that night to share with friends and it's even more special if I can actually harvest some of the ingredients from my own garden.

Remembering too that this is an equinox and balance is important we also should identify what is keeping us stuck or what we don't require in our lives any more and put some energy towards letting those things go or changing them.

LAMMAS

Our ancestors would have loved to celebrate Lammas – after all, here is a festival praising the bounty that hard work and nature provided. Lammas, or Lughnasadh (pronounced loog-na-sa), is a harvest festival, and since the people of this time could only rely on what the earth provided for them there was much joy and feelings of gratitude for what could be shared.

Gratitude is more than a modern buzzword. True gratitude signifies a real reciprocity, a giving and taking and a deep connective synergy. It is feeling a sense of gratitude for what we have, what we have earned and learned and even what possibilities we may have ahead of us. Getting into the habit of expressing our gratitude for all we have in life is a positive practice that influences everything from our mental state to the way we relate to others.

HOW TO CELEBRATE LAMMAS

If we sat down and listed everything that we have achieved and experienced in the past 12 months it could be seen as our personal harvest for the year. Take stock of this and be thankful. Think about where you are in life right now, because this is where you start. If you have an altar, the traditional colours are gold, brown and orange and offerings can include cider, mead, apples and baked goods.

I think you'll be happy to hear that Lammas is a time of feasting! This festival is a wonderful excuse to invite all your friends around and bake up big. As with all kitchen magic, be sure to stir in good vibes and wishes.

MABON
AUTUMN EQUINOX

Mabon, whilst being a harvest festival, being an equinox signals a balance of sorts. This is one of two times of the year when the balance of light and dark, (night and day) are equal. Yet, from the next day the light begins to recede and the days shorten. It's a time to seek balance in as many areas of our life as we can before the colder and darker times begin.

Within the wheel of the year, Mabon celebrated the second or last harvest for that growing season. The people knew that after this last taking of produce from the land, there would not be another chance until spring and so the fertility of the land was honoured. Communities worked together and what was harvested was seen as precious with every grain counted and stored and fruits preserved where possible. The last hunting parties before the harsh winter weather would be sent out. Gratitude for what was available was a central tenet of the festival and it was a social time when news was exchanged and matches arranged.

HOW TO CELEBRATE MABON

Like Lammas, Mabon is a time to recognise the harvest of our life and to be grateful for what we have. That could be something very simple – that we have food to eat, we are alive and healthy, that we see a beautiful flower on the way to work or a cute dog on the street. As such I always try and cook something special that night to share with friends and it's even more special if I can actually harvest some of the ingredients from my own garden.

Remembering too that this is an equinox and balance is important we also should identify what is keeping us stuck or what we don't require in our lives any more and put some energy towards letting those things go or changing them.

What you might like to try is a Mabon Spiral to celebrate Mabon. Gather things you find beautiful in a basket: flowers, crystals, leaves and also some apples, fruits, raw grains, even small pieces of paper with words you love on it – anything that suggests full harvest to you. Now take a breath and connect with the earth, this earth who is the embodiment of the goddess and who gives us all we really need. Allow your energies to mix. As you walk outwards step by step in a spiral shape place each item on the ground. After a few rounds of circular steps, you'll find you have been creating a beautiful sacred spiral. Look how lucky you are to have such a harvest! Your basket is empty. Thank the goddess! Now walk the spiral inwards, signifying the harvest and the coming of the colder times, and as you do pick up the items in your basket (leave some if you wish as gifts for the earth). Enjoy your harvest!

REFERENCES

ON SLEEP

Here's What Happens When You Don't Get Enough Sleep

https://health.clevelandclinic.org/happens-body-dont-get-enough-sleep/

LIST OF DELPHIC MAXIMS

147 Delphic maxims as cited by Stobaeus

1. Follow God
2. Obey the law
3. Worship the gods
4. Respect your parents
5. Be overcome by justice
6. Know what you have learned
7. Perceive what you have heard
8. Be (or know) yourself
9. Intend to get married
10. Know your opportunity
11. Think as a mortal
12. If you are a stranger, act like one
13. Honour the hearth (or Hestia)
14. Control yourself
15. Help your friends
16. Control anger
17. Exercise prudence
18. Honour providence
19. Do not use an oath
20. Love friendship
21. Cling to discipline
22. Pursue honour
23. Long for wisdom
24. Praise the good
25. Find fault with no one
26. Praise virtue
27. Practise what is just
28. Be kind to friends
29. Watch out for your enemies
30. Exercise nobility of character
31. Shun evil
32. Be impartial
33. Guard what is yours

34. Shun what belongs to others
35. Listen to everyone
36. Be (religiously) silent
37. Do a favour for a friend
38. Nothing to excess
39. Use time sparingly
40. Foresee the future
41. Despise insolence
42. Have respect for suppliants
43. Be accommodating in everything
44. Educate your sons
45. Give what you have
46. Fear deceit
47. Speak well of everyone
48. Be a seeker of wisdom
49. Choose what is divine
50. Act when you know
51. Shun murder
52. Pray for things possible
53. Consult the wise
54. Test the character
55. Give back what you have received
56. Down look no one
57. Use your skill
58. Do what you mean to do
59. Honour a benefaction
60. Be jealous of no one
61. Be on your guard
62. Praise hope
63. Despise a slanderer
64. Gain possessions justly
65. Honour good men
66. Know the judge

67. Master wedding feasts
68. Recognise fortune
69. Flee a pledge
70. Speak plainly
71. Associate with your peers
72. Govern your expenses
73. Be happy with what you have
74. Revere a sense of shame
75. Fulfil a favour
76. Pray for happiness
77. Be fond of fortune
78. Observe what you have heard
79. Work for what you can own
80. Despise strife
81. Detest disgrace
82. Restrain the tongue
83. Keep yourself from insolence
84. Make just judgements
85. Use what you have
86. Judge incorruptibly
87. Accuse one who is present
88. Tell when you know
89. Do not depend on strength
90. Live without sorrow
91. Live together meekly
92. Finish the race without shrinking back
93. Deal kindly with everyone
94. Do not curse your sons
95. Rule your wife
96. Benefit yourself
97. Be courteous
98. Give a timely response
99. Struggle with glory
100. Act without repenting
101. Repent of sins
102. Control the eye
103. Give a timely counsel
104. Act quickly
105. Guard friendship
106. Be grateful
107. Pursue harmony

108. Keep deeply the top secret
109. Fear ruling
110. Pursue what is profitable
111. Accept due measure
112. Do away with enmities
113. Accept old age
114. Do not boast in might
115. Exercise (religious) silence
116. Flee enmity
117. Acquire wealth justly
118. Do not abandon honour
119. Despise evil
120. Venture into danger prudently
121. Do not tire of learning
122. Do not stop to be thrifty
123. Admire oracles
124. Love whom you rear
125. Do not oppose someone absent
126. Respect the elder
127. Teach a youngster
128. Do not trust wealth
129. Respect yourself
130. Do not begin to be insolent
131. Crown your ancestors
132. Die for your country
133. Do not be discontented by life
134. Do not make fun of the dead
135. Share the load of the unfortunate
136. Gratify without harming
137. Grieve for no one
138. Beget from noble routes
139. Make promises to no one
140. Do not wrong the dead
141. Be well off as a mortal
142. Do not trust fortune
143. As a child be well behaved
144. As a youth be self-disciplined
145. As of middle age be just
146. As an old man be sensible
147. On reaching the end be without sorrow

Additional maxims, most likely local variants, have been identified from various sources including:

4. Obey the virtuous

11. Live without sorrow

13. Avoid the unjust

14. Testify what is right

15. Control pleasure

22. Praise virtue

27. Train your relatives

55. Believe in time

56. Receive for the pleasure

57. Prostrate before the divine

60. Do not boast in might

62. Use the one who has the same interests as you

64. Be embarrassed to lie

66. If you believe in something do not be scared to act for it

68. Be firm on what has been agreed

GENDERED HOUSEWORK: SPOUSAL RELATIVE INCOME, PARENTHOOD AND TRADITIONAL

Gender Identity Norms

Joanna Syrda

https://www.washingtonpost.com/lifestyle/2022/05/02/housework-divide-working-parents/

https://doi.org/10.1177/09500170211069780

ON OLYMPIANS

A Medal in the Olympics Runs in the Family: A Cohort Study of Performance Heritability in the Games History

https://www.ncbi.nlm.nih.gov/pmc/articles/PMC6157334/?fbclid=IwAR3iAQEjOd28-qzSKl9nEtb8wi8YUF91cPUTo6VV54kVrpsB3IquJBIonUY

ON VESTALS AND FAMILY RELATIONSHIPS

Vestal Virgins and Their Families

https://conservancy.umn.edu/bitstream/handle/11299/214958/Gallia-Vestals-Families.pdf?sequence=1

ABOUT THE
AUTHOR

Stacey Demarco is The Modern Witch. Passionate about bringing practical magic to everyone and inspiring people to have a deeper and more direct relationship with nature, she has been a pagan educator for many decades. She has a deep love for mythos and the use of natural cycles for greater success and connection.

She is the author of the bestselling books *Witch in the Boardroom*, *Witch in the Bedroom* and *The Enchanted Moon* and numerous beautiful oracle decks including the Amazon number ones *Queen of the Moon Oracle* and *The Elemental Oracle*. Her annual *Lunar & Seasonal Diary* is now in its 14th edition and is available in both southern and northern hemisphere editions. She leads the popular practical workshops Wild Souls Retreats and is available at times for one-on-one personal consults. Each year she runs a Zoom-based live version of *Priestess Path* for those who would like to work the 13 steps with others.

Stacey lives on a cliff by the beach in Sydney, Australia with her husband, furry companions and about 25,000 bees.

Learn more at themodernwitch.com, Stacey Demarco on Facebook or @themodernwitch on Instagram.